MADONNA

SONG BY SONG

MARC ANDREWS

FONTHILL

Fonthill Media Language Policy

Fonthill Media publishes in the international English language market. One language edition is published worldwide. As there are minor differences in spelling and presentation, especially with regard to American English and British English, a policy is necessary to define which form of English to use. The Fonthill Policy is to use the form of English native to the author. Marc Andrews was born and educated in Australia; therefore Australian English has been adopted in this publication.

Fonthill Media Limited
Fonthill Media LLC
www.fonthill.media

First published in the United Kingdom and the United States of America 2022
Reprinted 2024

British Library Cataloguing in Publication Data:
A catalogue record for this book is available from the British Library

Typeset in 10pt on 13pt Sabon
Printed and bound in England

Thanks and Dedication

'Take a Bow'

*Special thanks to Ian Cole for letting me part of his ABBA:
Song By Song book project and giving me the impetus and inspiration to write
this book!*

*Mike Bartsch for being a mega DDR pop fan. Madonna,
grant me the serenity—I wish I had gone to Melbourne with you in
March 2016. Es tut mir leid.*

*And—finally enough love!—to my husband, Uday, whose favourite Madonna
song is 'Holiday' because it always makes him feel happy. Like he does for me.*

This book is dedicated to Madonna, who taught me how to … ohhhhh!

Acknowledgements
'Keep It Together'

My very first Madonna record was a 12″, not because size mattered to me, but because it was given to me by my first boyfriend. The 'Like a Virgin' 12″, that is. We would never be apart again after that, Madonna and me, which is probably why my boyfriend got jealous and broke up with us—er, me. Madonna has been my constant companion, muse, inspiration, and the musical soundtrack for the entirety of my working life as a music and entertainment journalist.

My objective with *Madonna: Song by Song* was for it to be as accurate as possible, as factual as possible, and as interesting as possible. I also wanted to make sure it was not just written from an aloof music journalist's perspective, or an academic's dry, emotionless appraisal, but that it reflected a Madonna fan's love, appreciation, and admiration for her body of work—the great, the good and the downright 'I'm Going Bananas'. Oh, and if Madonna calls, tell her, I'm right here!

Contents

'Give It 2 Me'

Introduction

"You're a superstar/Yes, that's what you are/You know it"

"Vogue" (1990)

Growing up in America's conservative Midwest during the 1960s and early 1970s, no one expected, or could have predicted, Madonna Louise Veronica Ciccone would grow up to be a trailblazing global superstar, icon, and legend—except perhaps for Madonna herself.

In January 1984, during an *American Bandstand* TV performance to promote her breakthrough hit, 'Holiday', twenty-five-year-old upstart Madonna informed host Dick Clark her plan was 'to rule the world'. Little did anyone suspect she was already well on her way.

After a few years of trying to get a leg up as both a disco dancer in Paris and a new-wave punk rock singer in New York, Madonna eventually forged her own path that was a little bit of both, creating her own immaculate musical creation.

Signed to a deal by Seymour Stein to his Sire Records, a small subsidiary label with a worldwide major distribution deal with Warner Bros. Records, Madonna joined lauded label mates The Ramones, Talking Heads, and The Pretenders on the eclectic roster. Having moved to New York City in 1978 with $35 in her pocket, she had a lot to prove to herself and to those who had put their faith, and money, in her.

The first Madonna single in October 1982 was not actually a 7″ vinyl single at all, but a 12″ vinyl release of her self-penned new-wave dance track 'Everybody', produced by then boyfriend DJ Mark Kamins, the man who originally presented her demo to Stein. Though 'Everybody' failed to reach the Top 100 in the US, it peaked at #3 on *Billboard*'s Dance Club Songs chart, a listing that would prove to have an undying love affair with Madonna throughout her long and varied career. A follow-up 12″ was released in March 1983 boasting the double A-side of the self-penned 'Burning Up' and 'Physical Attraction', written for her by R&B producer Reggie Lucas. Again reaching #3 on the US Dance Club Songs chart, the doubleheader also accorded Madonna her first international hit in far-flung Australia, off the back of video play for 'Burning Up'.

An album was eventually commissioned by Sire with Lucas brought in to produce it, though Madonna later corralled her new boyfriend, DJ John "Jellybean" Benitez, to remix the tracks to make them more to her liking for its July 1983 release. Jellybean also brought with him to the project a new song selected as the album's first proper single in September that year, 'Holiday'. A joyous unity anthem that has refused to dim over the decades, 'Holiday' accorded Madonna her first Top 40 hit in the US, her first US Dance Club Songs #1, her first UK Top 10 hit, her first Australian Top 10 hit, and her first global #1 in a country that had only just come into existence, Zimbabwe.

The hits from her self-titled debut kept coming and they kept getting bigger and bigger. 'Borderline', again written for Madonna by Lucas, was her first US Top 10 hit, then the self-penned follow-up 'Lucky Star' became her first US Top 5 hit. All of this extended chart action meant Madonna's sophomore album had to be pushed back to later in 1984, but it was worth the wait. Released within weeks of each other towards the end of that year, the 'Like a Virgin' single and album both rushed to #1 around the globe and Madonnamania, via hordes of Madonna 'wannabes', was fully unleashed. With 1985's The Virgin Tour, it literally exploded.

Parallel to her burgeoning music career, Madonna was keen to start a movie career as an actor. Her cameo as a barroom singer in 1985's *Vision Quest* spawned two hits: her first ballad chart-topper in 'Crazy for You', which knocked USA For Africa's 'We Are The World' from the #1 perch in her homeland, and the rockier 'Gambler'.

A meatier role was presented to her in the indie flick *Desperately Seeking Susan*, a surprise box office hit that same year. It featured another Madonna tune, the irrepressible 'Into the Groove', written and produced by Madonna with her ex-boyfriend/former Breakfast Club bandmate Stephen Bray. Performed live during her three-track gig during the global *Live Aid* concert event in July 1985, after The Virgin Tour concluded, it sent Madonnamania into the stratosphere. At one point in the UK charts Madonna had the #1 single with 'Into the Groove' and #2 with the rereleased 'Holiday'. She managed even more hits that year with 'Material Girl', 'Angel', and 'Dress You Up' all from the mega-selling *Like a Virgin* album, while Sire/Warner cannily remarketed her eponymously titled debut album as *The First Album* with a more recent photo—bangles, crucifixes, hair extensions, and all—to incite her fervent wannabes even further.

On 16 August 1985, her twenty-seventh birthday and a month after *Live Aid*, Madonna married her movie star *beau* Sean Penn. While the marriage, and the movie they made together, 1986's *Shanghai Surprise*, were both relative disasters, he would inspire some of Madonna's finest, if not saddest, work.

Her stunning 1986 ballad 'Live to Tell', co-written and produced with her The Virgin Tour musical director Patrick Leonard, was not just the lead single from her third album, *True Blue*, dedicated to her beloved husband, of course, but also used on the soundtrack to his movie *At Close Range*. The global success of *True Blue* (selling upwards of 25 million copies worldwide) and its subsequent singles—'Papa Don't Preach', the title track, 'Open Your Heart', and 'La Isla Bonita'—went some way to making up for the box office disaster that was *Shanghai Surprise*.

While 'Like a Virgin' had stirred some notoriety for its then risqué title, and the publication of old nude photos in *Playboy* and *Penthouse* magazines also became front page news, it was not until 'Papa Don't Preach' that controversy formed an integral part of the ongoing Madonna story too. Pro-life and pro-choice lobbies both claimed the song about teen pregnancy as their own, while Madonna let the music speak for itself as it topped the charts and her music video ruled MTV.

Refusing to give up on her dream of acting stardom in addition to pop fame (if not infamy now), Madonna made her theatrical debut in *Goose and Tom-Tom* alongside her husband. She next took the lead in a screwball comedy that proved to be a bigger hit for her in the music charts than at the box office. *Who's That Girl* (1987) spawned three Madonna hits—the title track, 'Causing a Commotion', and 'The Look of Love'—and her first world tour, while the year ended with the first compilation of her work, party hard remix album *You Can Dance*.

The year 1989 was to prove a momentous, if not a critical turning point for Madonna. Coming from a self-described 'dark place', she poured the anguish about her disintegrating marriage into her music, delivering her first profoundly personal record. The 'Like a Prayer' single and album were not only huge commercial hits, but also, for the first time in her career, critically acclaimed. As with most things that provocateur Madonna manhandled, however, controversy was never far away. A multi-million dollar deal with Pepsi was abandoned after the storm over her 'Like a Prayer' video brought her condemnation from religious groups and even the Vatican, a good Catholic girl like Madonna's worst nightmare. Yet while Madonna seemed to be forever in the headlines, her music remained top of the charts. 'Express Yourself', 'Cherish', 'Dear Jessie', 'Oh Father', and 'Keep It Together' were all hits culled from *Like a Prayer*.

Post-divorce Madonna threw herself into her next major movie role in *Dick Tracy*, which also resulted in a romance with the movie's star, director, and producer, perpetual Hollywood womanizer Warren Beatty. An album combining songs written for the film by musical theatre legend Stephen Sondheim, and Madonna/Patrick Leonard collabs inspired by the movie, arrived in 1990 called *I'm Breathless*.

Yet it was a small underground dance track, which Madonna had put together on the side with her favourite remixer, Shep Pettibone, which supplied the album's first single. 'Vogue' was not just a global #1 hit, a million seller, and brought the gay dance trend to the mainstream, it became another signature Madonna song and music video.

The racy 'Hanky Panky' became the second and final hit from *I'm Breathless* as Madonna toured the world on her Blond Ambition World Tour—now considered one of, if not the greatest arena shows ever put on by a pop act.

By the end of 1990, Madonna's romance to Warren Beatty had also come to an end as she released her second compilation, *The Immaculate Collection*, featuring two new songs, 'Justify My Love' and 'Rescue Me'. Controversy again stirred due to the omnisexual activity in her too-hot-for-MTV 'Justify My Love' video, but Madonna laughed off the ban all the way to the bank via video sales.

If 'Justify My Love' had raised eyebrows, her next venture raised not only many libidos but much religious ire. Releasing a book of her sexual fantasies in 1992, simply called *Sex*, Madonna pushed more buttons than she even knew existed. Sadly, the fallout and furore over Madonna's venture into coffee-table porn publishing smothered the release of the accompanying album, *Erotica*, mostly co-written and co-produced by Pettibone and his then partner Tony Shimkin. 'Deeper and Deeper', 'Bad Girl', 'Fever', 'Rain', and 'Bye Bye Baby' were all much smaller hits than they should have been. Her movie career also lurched in fits and starts—1992's *A League of Their Own* (featuring the gorgeous 'This Used to be My Playground') was a major hit, but 1993's *Body of Evidence* was widely panned. Still, her record label, Maverick, set up in 1992, proved to be adept at sourcing talent and struck multi-platinum with Alanis Morrissette's *Jagged Little Pill* in 1995 becoming the decade's biggest selling album.

In 1994, after dating both basketballer Dennis Rodman and rapper Tupac Shakur, Madonna shrewdly switched genres releasing an R&B album, *Bedtime Stories*, to woo back her audience in a less threatening manner. While 'Secret' and 'Take a Bow' were major hits—'Take a Bow' taking the honour of being her longest running US #1—subsequent singles, 'Bedtime Story' and 'Human Nature', flopped at home, although globally they sold well.

Madonna had bigger matters on her mind though—she had finally nabbed the role of a lifetime as Eva Peron in the film musical version of *Evita*. Taking time out from prepping, she recorded three new songs for 1995's ballads compilation, *Something to Remember,* mixing power ballad ('You'll See') with cutting edge ('I Want You').

Evita was not the only big thing looming on the horizon for Madonna. A few months prior to the release of the movie in December 1996, Madonna gave birth to her first child, Lourdes, fathered by her personal trainer boyfriend Carlos Leon.

The year 1997 saw *Evita* become a huge box office hit, new mother Madonna win a Golden Globe as Best Actress for her role and soundtrack hits 'You Must

Love Me', 'Don't Cry For Me Argentina', and 'Another Suitcase In Another Hall' cement her position as the undisputed 'Queen of Pop'.

Teaming up with experimental pop eccentric William Orbit for 1998's *Ray of Light* album, Madonna was rewarded not only with a slew of hit singles ('Frozen', the title track, 'The Power of Good-bye', 'Drowned World/Substitute for Love', and 'Nothing Really Matters') and the best reviews of her career, but a bucketful of Grammy awards for the first time too.

Madonna's career had never been in better shape—nor had she, thanks to her physically punishing yoga routines and Kabbalah inspired mindfulness. After soundtrack success with 'Beautiful Stranger' from the 1999 box office hit *Austin Powers: The Spy Who Shagged Me* and 'American Pie' from 2000's box office flop *The Next Best Thing*, which she starred in alongside BFF Rupert Everett, Madonna had also found success in love again, this time with British director Guy Ritchie.

They married in December 2000 a few months after Madonna gave birth to her second child, a son called Rocco, and released her #1 'Music' single and electropop-folk hybrid album. Spawning two more hits in 'Don't Tell Me' and 'What it Feels like for a Girl', and 2001's hugely successful Drowned World Tour, Madonna and husband Ritchie teamed up for a car commercial, a music video, and a movie. Well, two out of three ain't bad. Their 2002 bomb, *Swept Away*, is considered one of the worst movies of all time and fairly much killed off any acting ambitions Madonna may have had left.

Faced with a stalled movie career, Madonna focused on what Madonna did best—making music and cooking up controversies to go with them. Point in question—2003's *American Life* album, which caused such grave political fallout during the Iraqi War that Madonna's career, certainly at conservative radio in the US, never fully recovered. Much like she did after the *Sex* book sank her *Erotica* album, Madonna, now a UK resident who wrote children's books in her spare time, pressed on and turned to the world's favourite classic pop band, ABBA, for help. 'Hung Up' (2005), which sampled the super Swedes, saw her back in favour with the accompanying retro-disco *Confessions on a Dance Floor* album pleasing fans and foes alike. Her 2006's Confessions Tour—her third tour already that decade after 2001's Drowned World Tour and 2004's Re-Invention World Tour—was another colossal hit and further proof if ever it was needed that Madonna was simply the greatest entertainer on the planet.

That year, together with Ritchie, she adopted her third child, David, from Malawi, which led to Madonna's philanthropic work in the tiny African country. The 2008 documentary *I Am Because We Are* focused on her humanitarian work, as opposed to 1991's *Truth or Dare: In Bed with Madonna* and 2005's *I'm Going to Tell You a Secret* docos, which focused primarily on Madonna, and her music, of course.

The year 2008 was pivotal for Mrs Ritchie. She recorded her last album under her Sire/Warner Bros contract, the urban-inclined *Hard Candy*, with the help of super producer Timbaland and super popstar Justin Timberlake (the ex of Britney Spears who Madonna famously smooched live on MTV in 2003). Madonna was also inducted into the Rock and Roll Hall of Fame and directed her first film, *Filth & Wisdom*. If all that seemed like a lot—Madonna is superhuman for a good reason—she was also in the process of divorcing second husband Ritchie.

Now, in 2009, single mother Ms. Ciccone released *Celebration*, her fourth compilation album (after 1990's *The Immaculate Collection*, 1995's *Something To Remember*, and 2001's *GHV2*) and yet still found time to adopt another child, Mercy, from Malawi.

For the next two years, Madonna turned her attention to directing the period drama *W.E.*, based on the love story between English King Edward VIII and American Wallis Simpson. She also shifted focus from the music business to business ventures—namely the Material Girl clothing line with daughter Lourdes, the Hard Candy Fitness gym chain, and her own Truth or Dare lifestyle brand.

The year 2012 finally saw her welcome return to music with the release of her twelfth studio album, launched with a show-stopping half-time performance during that year's Super Bowl including her new single 'Give Me All Your Luvin'', her final US Top 10 single to date. The new album, *MDNA*, her first with her new label Interscope Records, also witnessed the welcome return of William Orbit as a writer/producer on the project, although he endured a social media falling out with Madonna soon after the album's release and was banished thereafter.

Despite the *MDNA* album suffering from the dreaded monster of ageism in pop music, the accompanying MDNA Tour proved a huge money-spinner. Madonna gave back a year later in 2013 through her Raising Malawi foundation building ten schools in the country and also donating money to her Detroit hometown to help it out of bankruptcy. That year she also launched her luxe MDNA Skin line, though there were noticeable rumblings amongst Madonna fans that Madonna herself no longer looked like the Madonna of old and this was not all down to an overpriced skin care range.

That was a minor complaint compared to what Madonna had to endure at the end of 2014—the leak of not just her entire new album, but most of the demo versions and additional songs too in a few well-orchestrated internet dumps. Long blighted during her career by web leaks, the *Rebel Heart* debacle led to a prison sentence for the culprit, but also severely impacted the album's chart performance, single releases and critical reception. A global tour was again a huge financial success, and well-reviewed, but in the midst of that huge undertaking Madonna became embroiled in a bitter and very public custody battle with ex-husband Ritchie over their son Rocco.

Madonna's secret *Tears of a Clown* show for fans in March 2016 in Melbourne was one of the few times the superstar had ever let down her guard as she dealt with the prospect of being a mother not allowed to have contact with her child. The matter was eventually resolved out of court and the following year Madonna adopted Malawi toddler twins Estere and Stella to add to her brood as she took a break from music for four years, later controversially labelling what had happened to her with the *Rebel Heart* leaks 'terrorism' and 'rape'.

Moving from New York to Lisbon, Portugal, to support son David's professional soccer playing ambitions, Madonna was influenced by the city's fado music, which would come alive to infuse 2019's *Madame X* album. Launched with the Maluma duet 'Medellín', the album garnered her best reviews in two decades and led to the innovative Madame X Tour at smaller venues in a handful of cities in the US and Europe. She returned to the spotlight and charts in mid-2020 for a guest spot on Dua Lipa's 'Levitating' hit also featuring Missy Elliott, plus *Billboard* ranked her the #1 greatest music video artist of all time.

Now, forty years after making her first record, Madonna can already reflect on a career not just as a dancer, musician, singer, actor, performer, provocateur, rebel, director, entrepreneur, philanthropist, and mother, but also as a gifted songwriter/producer who changed the world, one smash hit at a time.

This book is Madonna's superstar journey told through the magic of her music and the gift of her songs. 'Don't just stand there … let's get to it!'

About Madonna's Recordings 'Has to Be'

From her first US release on Sire/Warner Bros. Records, as a solo artist under her own name, Madonna has recorded and officially released well over 250 songs. They are spread across fourteen studio albums *(Madonna, Like a Virgin, True Blue, Like a Prayer, Erotica, Bedtime Stories, Ray of Light, Music, American Life, Confessions on a Dance Floor, Hard Candy, MDNA, Rebel Heart, and Madame X)*, four soundtrack albums *(Who's That Girl, I'm Breathless: Music From and Inspired by the film Dick Tracy, Evita, and The Next Best Thing)*, four compilations *(The Immaculate Collection, Something to Remember, GHV2, and Celebration)*, three remix albums *(You Can Dance, Remixed & Revisited, and Confessions Remixed)* and a number of non-album 7″ single, 12″ extended, maxi B-sides, and EPs (extended plays). Additionally, there are six official live releases *(I'm Going To Tell You A Secret, The Confessions Tour, Sticky & Sweet Tour, MDNA World Tour, Rebel Heart Tour, and Madame X: Music From The Theater Xperience)*.

All songs listed are solo works by Madonna unless otherwise indicated, while all albums and single releases carry their US label catalogue numbers unless otherwise noted.

Because so many individual Madonna tracks have so many variations on their running length due to edits, radio edits and various remix edits, the listings in this book generally refer to the standard album release duration/length, or their according single variation if applicable.

All songs have for the most part been listed chronologically in order of their release in each corresponding book chapter/era. In general, only songs that have been officially released have been listed, although some exceptions have been included. Any Madonna music of note that is unreleased, unofficial, featured live or in live recordings, or widely reported/rumoured, is listed in Appendix I.

1

The Madonna Era

Madonna
Sire: 92-3867-1
Released: July 1983
Side A

'Lucky Star'	5:30
'Borderline'	5:18
'Burning Up'	4:48
'I Know It'	3:45

Side B

'Holiday'	6:08
'Think Of Me'	4:53
'Physical Attraction'	6:35
'Everybody'	4:47

'Everybody'

Sire: 0-29899-0 A **12″ release:** October 1982 **Album:** *Madonna*
Writer: Madonna
Producer: Mark Kamins

'My whole career started out with 12 inches,' Madonna once famously declared, 'some girls have all the luck!' 'Everybody', on 12″ vinyl, is the song that started it all for the Queen of Pop. Madonna's debut 12″ was originally recorded as a demo with her ex, Stephen Bray of The Breakfast Club. Thanks to her persistent pestering, DJ Mark Kamins spun it at New York's Danceteria venue. Not just a DJ, Kamins brought it to Sire Records, an offshoot of Warner Bros. Label boss Seymour Stein signed Madonna before being discharged from hospital. While Kamins is credited as producer, studio boffin Arthur Baker mentored him, tapping synth maestro Fred Zarr. The 'Everybody' 12″ cover art was a Lou Beach hip-hop style collage of an NYC street scene to disguise the fact Madonna was white. The final song on her eight-track eponymous debut album, and a #3 US club hit, when Kamins died in 2013, Madonna paid tribute to him stating: 'if it weren't for him, I might not have had a singing career. He was the first DJ to play my demos before I had a record deal. He believed in me before anyone else did. I owe him a lot'.

Vid Bit!

Director: Ed Steinberg

Steinberg launched the RockAmerica music video subscription service for DJs. 'Everybody' is not so much low-budget as no-budget ($1,500).

Remix Fix!

Visage's Rusty Egan crafted a shoutier mix of 'Everybody' for the UK market.

'Burning Up'

Sire: 0-29715 **12″ release:** March 1983 (US) **7″ release:** October 1983 (Australia)
Album: *Madonna*
Writer: Madonna
Producer: Reggie Lucas

A major club hit in the US together with 'Physical Attraction', in a pairing one critic decreed 'electroporn', 'Burning Up' was also a Top 20 hit single in Australia thanks to heavy video rotation. 'Burning Up' boasted Madonna's first video-with-a-budget and first remix too, both which would be *de rigueur* from then on. Composed back in 1980 when she was part of the band Emmy and solely credited to Madonna, its Warholian cover art, designed by her gay BFF Martin Burgoyne, showcased Madonna styled by fashion influencer/artist Maripol. Madonna's punky dance anthem has since been thrashed through by Iggy Pop and the Stooges in 2008 during her induction during the Rock and Roll Hall of Fame, included as a bonus track on 2010's *Glee: The Music, The Power of Madonna* #1 US soundtrack album and covered live by Britney Spears on 2011's Femme Fatale Tour.

Vid Bit!

Director: Steve Barron

Time for a proper Madonna video from the man who directed Michael Jackson's 'Billie Jean', arranged courtesy of their shared manager at the time, Freddy DeMann.

Remix Fix!

In-demand NYC DJ Jellybean added crunchy guitars and extra vocals to Lucas' original disco-goes-punk 'Burning Up'.

'Physical Attraction'

Sire: 9 29715-0 A **12″ release:** March 1983 (US) **7″ release:** October 1983 (Australia) **Album:** *Madonna*
Writer/Producer: Reggie Lucas

Sultry, sensual, and redressing disco in a post-punk electro sheen, 'Physical Attraction' was the first of two Lucas compositions destined for the *Madonna* album after initially being issued as a double-A 12″ with 'Burning Up'. Respected jazz musician Lucas was hot chart property after crafting R&B/disco hits for Roberta Flack, Phyllis Hyman and Stephanie Mills (whose 1980 single 'Sweet Sensation' is doubtlessly where 'Physical Attraction' was cloned from). He surely sensed some sexual chemistry, writing 'Physical Attraction' after witnessing Madonna perform live. A true mix of street sounds and new wave, Lucas called his work with Madonna 'a crossover pop record of the highest order'.

'Lucky Star'

Sire: 7-29177 **Single release:** September 1983/June 1984 **Album:** *Madonna*
Writer: Madonna
Producers: Reggie Lucas, Jellybean

The timeless, iconic, and funky 'Lucky Star' became Madonna's first Top 5 US hit delaying the release of her next album, *Like a Virgin*. 'Lucky Star' was only released as a single because she needed money to quash some costly lawsuits. Boy, did that pay off! Performed on numerous Madonna live shows, arguably most memorably melded with 'Hung Up' on her Confessions Tour, 'Lucky Star' is after 'Material Girl' the song title most attributed to Madonna during her early years.

Vid Bit!

Director: Arthur Pierson

Shot in one afternoon with Madonna, brother Christopher Ciccone, and pal Erika Belle. Warner Bros. exec Jeff Ayeroff bragged he 'made "Lucky Star" for $14,000 with a friend who was a pot grower'.

Remix Fix!

Jellybean was allowed to tinker with 'Lucky Star' to make it more to Madonna's liking, crucial as he was dating her at the time of its single release.

'Borderline'

Sire: 0-20212 **Single release:** February 1984 **Album:** *Madonna*
Writer/Producer: Reggie Lucas

'"Physical Attraction" and "Borderline" were done specifically during the production process and for her,' Lucas later recalled of his two *Madonna* contributions. 'Borderline' is easily the sweetest, most traditional style pop song on Madonna's debut album. Released as the fourth, or fifth single, in some territories, 'Borderline' became her first US Top 10 hit and a hit twice in the UK (#56 in 1984 and #2 when rereleased in 1986). In 2016, Madonna performed 'Borderline' live in front of US President Barack Obama on *The Tonight Show Starring Jimmy Fallon*.

Vid Bit!

Director: Mary Lambert

'Borderline' is where the Madonna magic perfectly translated to the medium of music video in a beautiful consensual relationship that continues to this day. Madonna's on-screen latino boyfriend, Louie Louie, claimed they were an item on set too.

Remix Fix!

A variety of remixes and dubs were swizzled by man-of-the-then-moment Jellybean.

'I Know It'

Release: July 1983 **Album:** *Madonna*
Writer: Madonna
Producer: Reggie Lucas

The sparse production on 'I Know It' is embellished by some welcome sax blasts, Fred Zarr's inventive synth playing and Madonna's dynamite knowing delivery. Globally it is estimated the *Madonna* album, which eventually hit the Top 10 in the US, UK, and Australia, has sold over 10 million copies. In 2020, *Pitchfork* ranked *Madonna* the #16 best album of the 1980s (*Like a Prayer* ranked #78 and *Like a Virgin* #115) affirming it, 'set the shimmying pace for a decade dripping in synths, drum machines and sex'.

'Holiday'

Sire: 7-29478 **Single release:** September 1983 **Album:** *Madonna*
Writers: Curtis Hudson, Lisa Stevens
Producer: John 'Jellybean' Benitez

The ultimate feel-good party anthem, Madonna's 'Holiday' is the song the world dances to when celebrating hope, happiness and harmony. A hit three times in the UK (1984, 1985, and 1991), her breakthrough Top 40 hit in the US (and first dance chart #1) and memorably warbled at 1985's *Live Aid* (and during eight of her concert tours), this proto-disco tune was dug up by DJ/boyfriend Jellybean. Written by members of black, post-disco act Pure Energy, 'Holiday' was turned down by both soul singer Phyllis Hyman and former Supremes singer Mary Wilson. After the addition of some memorable piano lines from Fred Zarr, 'Holiday' was delivered as Madonna's last-minute album replacement for the rudely yanked 'Ain't No Big Deal'. As the lead single from her self-titled debut album, it is fair to say 'Holiday' is the song that handed Madonna her career. In 2019, Madonna herself admitted 'Holiday' is so good a song it resists her constant attempts at reinventing it.

VID BIT!

While no official video for 'Holiday' was commissioned (though Ed Steinberg directed a less celebrated one for RockAmerica), the UK *Top of the Pops* performance was widely circulated by her record label.

REMIX FIX!

Although officially only Jellybean (for 1987's *You Can Dance* remix album) and Shep Pettibone (for 1990's *The Immaculate Collection)* have tackled 'Holiday', a white label bootleg interpolating *Holiday* with Stardust's 'Music Sounds Better With You' hit from 1998 was blocked from a proper release. A rap version, 'Holiday Rap', by Dutch duo MC Miker G & DJ Sven, hit the charts in 1986. Madonna, wisely, has never performed this version.

'Think of Me'

Release: July 1983 **Album:** *Madonna*
Writer: Madonna
Producer: Reggie Lucas

One of only two tracks on the Madonna album that did not see a single or 12″ release, Lucas brings 'Think of Me' alive as a piece of credible white girl R&B. 'Just for the record, one tires in a lifetime of hearing someone taking credit for something that you've done,' he complained. 'Jellybean produced "Holiday" and remixed a couple of tracks, but remixing tracks for radio isn't the same thing as producing one of the major breakout pop stars of the 1980s.' Picking up the tricks of the trade, from her third album onwards Madonna, always thinking ahead, became her own co-producer.

'Ain't No Big Deal'

Sire: 7599 20503-2 **Single release:** June 1986 (B-side to 'Papa Don't Preach')
Sire: 9 28591-7 September 1986 (B-side to 'True Blue')
Writer: Stephen Bray
Producer: Reggie Lucas

Originally planned for Madonna's debut album before being nixed at the last minute, 'Ain't No Big Deal' was considered the great lost Madonna 'killer B' side. Having initially been promised the chance to produce the song, her ex and demo partner Bray in a huff took ownership of 'Ain't No Big Deal' producing a version for disco act Barracuda thus precluding Madonna from using it. 'Ain't No Big Deal' had to wait until 1984 for a release on the Warner compilation *Revenge of the Killer B's*. As recorded by Lucas for Madonna's debut album, it gamely struggles to span the wide divide between disco and new wave punk. When Lucas died in 2018, Madonna paid tribute to him writing, 'so sad to hear that Reggie Lucas is gone … an important part of my musical past. RIP. #gratitude #luckystar.'

'Sidewalk Talk' (Jellybean)

EMI America: 12 EA 210 **12″ single release:** October 1984 **EP:** *Wotupski!?!*
Writer: Madonna
Producer: John "Jellybean" Benitez

While critics often insinuated Madonna used her 'boy toys' to kick-start her career in the music biz, it was not a one-way street, or sidewalk even. One of the great 'lost hits' of the 1980s, 'Sidewalk Talk' hit the pop charts in the midst of the global grip of Madonnamania. 'Sidewalk Talk' was credited to Jellybean, though the chorus vocals are unmistakably Madonna (with assistance from Catherine Buchanan). A US Top 20 hit that just missed the UK Top 40, Madonna gifted this freestyle synth-pop ode to her early days in NYC to boyfriend Jellybean's debut *Wotupski!?!* EP—then Sean Penn walked in.

2

The *Like a Virgin* Era

Like a Virgin
Sire: 9 25157-1
Released: November 1984
Side A

'Material Girl'	4:04
'Angel'	3:57
'Like A Virgin'	3:39
'Over and Over'	4:13
'Love Don't Live Here Anymore'	4:51

Side B

'Into The Groove'*	4:40
'Dress You Up'	4:02
'Shoo-Bee-Doo'	5:18
'Pretender'	4:31
'Stay'	4:09

*Added to the rereleased *Like a Virgin* album in 1985 in territories outside the US.

'Like a Virgin'

Sire: 0-20239 **Single release:** October 1984 **Album:** *Like a Virgin*
Writers: Tom Kelly, Billy Steinberg
Producer: Nile Rodgers

Madonna's first #1 single and first true signature song, 'Like a Virgin' is one of the classic pop songs of the 1980s, an enduring hit and a pop culture phenomenon. It transformed Madonna from a pop star to a superstar. The title track from her sophomore album was chosen by her record company after initially being written as a sensitive ballad. Madonna went 'crazy' hearing the song for the very first time, though Rodgers' first impression was 'retarded'. 'Like a Virgin' became Madonna's first US #1 single, a #1 in Australia, Canada, Japan and her biggest hit to that point in the UK at #3. The song's actual debut was at the inaugural *MTV Music Video Awards* where Madonna, in matching wedding dress and 'boy toy' belt, writhed shamelessly on the floor. 'Like a Virgin' is now listed in the Rock and Roll Hall of Fame as one of the '500 songs that shaped rock and roll'.

VID BIT!
Director: Mary Lambert

Filmed in Venice because, according to Lambert, 'the idea of Madonna singing in a gondola was the most outrageous thing I could think of', the 'Like a Virgin' video was voted by VH1 at one of the 100 Greatest Videos of all time (at #62).

REMIX FIX!
Boyfriend Jellybean was on remix duties for this big hair '80s Extended Dance Remix.

'Stay'

Release: November 1984 **Album:** *Like a Virgin*
Writers: Madonna, Stephen Bray
Producer: Nile Rodgers

The B-side to 'Like a Virgin' is an overlooked gem from Madonna's early career. On an album of hits mostly written by other people, the jaunty, sixties girl bop of 'Stay' is like a virginal precursor to 1986's *True Blue*. Rodgers bluntly described the *Like a Virgin* album in 2011 as 'the white-artist-singing-black music formula'. In 2019, Blondie's Debbie Harry infuriatedly pouted in her autobiography *Face It* she had worked with Rodgers on 1981's *KooKoo* album long before Rodgers-virgins Bowie and Madonna.

'Material Girl'

Sire: 7-29083 **Single release:** January 1985 **Album:** *Like a Virgin*
Writers: Peter Brown, Robert Rans
Producer: Nile Rodgers

How do you follow a colossal pop culture moment? With another one, of course! Though she later detested it, 'Material Girl' was meant ironically, hitting #2 in the US, #3 in the UK, and #4 in Australia. Despite her disdain for it, Madonna has performed 'Material Girl' on many of her tours, almost always reinventing it as a joke number. In 2010 Madonna launched the Material Girl fashion line with then teenage daughter Lourdes. Five years later, she told *US*

Weekly 'Material Girl' is her least favourite song adding, 'I never want to hear it again!'

VID BIT!

Director: Mary Lambert

Freshly reinvented, and not for the last time, blonde bombshell Madonna channelled Marilyn Monroe's performance of 'Diamonds are a Girl's Best Friend' from 1953's *Gentleman Prefer Blondes* movie for the 'Material Girl' video, alongside Oscar-winning actor/songwriter Keith Carradine. It was also on the video set where Madonna met Sean Penn for the first time.

REMIX FIX!

A distinctly 'trapped in the 80s' mix from the Madonna remix catalogue, courtesy of Jellybean.

'Angel'

Sire: 0-20335 **Single release:** April 1985 **Album:** *Like a Virgin*
Writers: Madonna, Stephen Bray
Producer: Nile Rodgers

Sandwiched between pop powerhouses 'Material Girl' and 'Like a Virgin' on her sophomore album, 'Angel' proved to be no slouch as its third single. 'Angel' reached #5 in both the UK and US, but became her first self-penned #1 in Australia. That may also have been something to do with 'Into the Groove' being on the B-side there. 'Angel' was, Madonna avowed, 'something that I felt when I was young. I thought it would make for an interesting story if I wrote that as a song on my record.'

VID BIT!

Her UK record company devilishly assembled a clip from previous Madonna videos.

REMIX FIX!

The Extended Dance Mix of 'Angel', by Nile Rodgers and James Farber, might just have the greatest opening to any Madonna remix ever—a cheering crowd chanting her name over and over. Truly angelic!

'Over and Over'

Release: November 1984 **Album:** *Like a Virgin*
Writers: Madonna, Stephen Bray
Producer: Nile Rodgers

Originally written by Madonna during her punk-rock days in 1981, Madonna sells 'Over and Over' as if her life depends upon it. Rodgers was later to comment about his then patron: 'I am always amazed by Madonna's incredible judgment when it comes to making pop records. I've never seen anyone do it better, and that's the truth. When we did that album, it was the perfect union, and I knew it from the first day in the studio. The thing between us, man, it was sexual, it was passionate, it was creativity … it was pop'.

Remix Fix!

Steve Thompson and Michael Barbiero remixed 'Over and Over' for 1987's *You Can Dance* remix album in pure mid-80s style.

'Love Don't Live Here Anymore'

Maverick: 9362-4369202 **Single release:** March 1996 **Album:** *Like a Virgin*
Writer: Miles Gregory
Producer: Nile Rodgers

A classic mellow hit in 1978 for disco outfit Rose Royce, Madonna's 'Love Don't Live Here Anymore' never strays too far from the original. In 1996, it became a loveless single choice, reworked as a cut from 1995's *Something to Remember* ballad compilation. Barely making a ripple in the US top 100 pre-*Evita,* 'LDLHA' became Madonna's smallest chart hit there to date. In 2020, Pitchfork reassessed the *Like a Virgin* album declaring Madonna 'sold ballads like her cover of 'LDLHA' with raw emotion rather than vocal power'.

Vid Bit!

Director: Jean-Baptiste Mondino

The 'Love Don't Live Here Anymore' video was shot in Buenos Aires in 1996 in one take on a day off from the *Evita* set. Pregnant with daughter Lourdes, that caused Madonna to keep forgetting the lyrics and delaying the shoot.

Remix Fix!

Twelve 'LDLHA' remixes, from Soulpower's plodding R&B (released on the CD single) to Mark Picchiotti and C.L. McSpadden/Markus Schulz's dubby house (promo-only), were planned for release as a Rhino digital album in 2021 then postponed.

'Dress You Up'

Sire: 7-28919 **Single release:** July 1985 **Album:** *Like a Virgin*
Writers: Andrea LaRusso, Peggy Stanziale
Producer: Nile Rodgers

For the final track selected for the *Like a Virgin* project, Rogers asked New Jersey songwriters LaRusso and Stanziale to compose a song for Madonna in the style of his band Chic. Another Madonna song considered 'vulgar' and 'filthy' by conservative US groups at the time, due to its subtle sexual connotations, 'Dress You Up' later led to the Parental Advisory stickers on records. A Top 5 hit in the US, UK, and Australia, 'Dress You Up' was incorporated a number of times into her live shows, while in 2015 Madonna hilariously warbled it as a 'Bathroom Concert Series' duet with Ellen DeGeneres.

VID BIT!
Director: Danny Kleinman

The 'Dress You Up' clip captures that glorious moment in time when 'Virginmania' had taken over the world and Madonna's bellybutton was the star of the show and her tour.

REMIX FIX!
Jellybean's 12″ Formal Mix and Casual Instrumental Mix were lovingly 'influenced' by New Order's 'Blue Monday' dancefloor destroyer from 1983.

'Shoo-Bee-Doo'

Release: November 1984 **Album:** *Like a Virgin*
Writer: Madonna
Producer: Nile Rodgers

This delightful doo-wop song deceptively begins as a piano ballad with Madonna cooing in turmoil ('I see so much confusion and it's killing me') before 'Shoo-Bee-Doo' amps up into a mid-tempo '80s power ballad. Credited solely to Madonna as songwriter, there's a seductive sax solo from *Saturday Night Live* band director Lenny Pickett that matches Madonna's pleading, anguished vocals. Sitting perched alongside *Like a Virgin*'s 'Stay', 'Pretender', and 'Angel', 'Shoo-Bee-Doo' completes a quartet of charming tunes clearly influenced by, and gushily in love with, '60s girl groups.

'Pretender'

Release: November 1985 **Album:** *Like a Virgin*
Writers: Madonna, Stephen Bray
Producer: Nile Rodgers

The B-side to 'Material Girl' is yet another 'True Blue' lite, as if Madonna had not quite gotten the blueprint right yet for her perfect '60s pastiche. 'When I was making the record, I was just so thrilled and happy to be working with Nile Rodgers,' she mused later. Like one of his late 1970s Sister Sledge productions transported to the Motown of the '60s with Madonna channelling Diana Ross (Rodgers famously produced her biggest selling single 'Upside Down' in 1980), 'Pretender' possesses one of Madonna's most unpretentious early vocals.

'Crazy for You'

Geffen Records: GEFA 6323 **Single release:** March 1985 **Soundtrack:** *Vision Quest/Crazy For You*
Writers: John Bettis, Jon Lind
Producer: Jellybean

In her first major Hollywood movie role Madonna's brief appearance as 'singer at the local bar' is *Vision Quest*'s only true bright spark. 'Crazy for You' was such a big hit it knocked USA for Africa's all-star charity single 'We Are the World' off the top spot in the US (letting Madonna have her revenge for not being asked to participate). In the UK it was even a hit twice—in 1985 and 1991. Despite both Jellybean and Madonna being out of their comfort zone on a ballad, 'Crazy for You' is now considered one of the greatest, if not sexiest, love songs of all time. On 2004's Re-Invention World Tour, Madonna graciously dedicated 'Crazy for You' to 'all my fans—thank you for sticking by me for all these years!'

VID BIT!
Director: Harold Becker

The best bits of *Vision Quest* in just over four minutes, here's iconic Madonna in her mid-80s glory. Little wonder the movie was later renamed *Crazy for You*!

REMIX FIX!
Junior Vasquez's Arena Anthem version has unofficially been floating around the internet for years, finally delivering 'Crazy for You' melodrama to the dance floor.

'Into the Groove'

Sire: 920 352-0 **Single release:** July 1985 **Album:** *Like a Virgin* (1985 reissue)
Writers/Producers: Madonna, Stephen Bray

Madonna's greatest dance song, if not the greatest dance hit ever? Quite possibly, until 'Vogue', 'Music', and 'Hung Up' all got their own groove on in years to come. 'Into the Groove' was written hurriedly with Bray before Madonna went out on a date with her hot Puerto Rican neighbour. This quintessential Madonna song wound up being folded into her then current movie project, *Desperately Seeking Susan*. Just like 'Crazy for You', the song became bigger than the movie itself and 'Into the Groove' certainly has had a lasting impact on popular culture, pop music and the emerging post-disco dance music scene. Used in the movie in—get this!—a club scene where Madonna steps to the beat, 'Into the Groove' embodies dance floor liberation and a call to all, especially minorities like the gay community, because only when you are dancing can you feel this free. Though later calling the song she initially wrote for Mark Kamins' *protégé* Chyne 'retarded', 'Into the Groove' gave Madonna her major breakthrough in the UK after warbling it on the *Live Aid* concerts in July 1985. At one stage, 'Into the Groove' was at #1—her first #1 of thirteen there—while 'Holiday' held at #2 in the UK chart, and it remains her biggest selling British hit to date at just under a million copies. In the US, *Billboard* magazine awarded it 'Dance Single of the Decade', while Dannii Minogue was permitted to sample Madonna's version for 2003's 'Don't Wanna Lose This Feeling' single. The self-penned and self-produced 'Into the Groove', added to later pressings of the *Like a Virgin* album, proved Madonna was already a pop icon. Good going, stranger!

Vid Bit!

Director: Susan Seidelman

Little more than desperately splicing scenes together from her movie, Seidelman at least took a creative approach to Madonna's video—'Into the Groove' even ends with her movie's breakout star picture in a heart-shape. In the movie itself, 'Into the Groove' was used in a club scene between Madonna and actor Mark Blum, one of the first celebrity deaths from COVID-19 in 2020.

Remix Fix!

Only available as the B-side to the 'Angel' 12″ single in the US, this is certainly Madonna's most influential, timeless, and admired dance song with pop crossover appeal. Shep Pettibone took a few bashes at it on 1987's *You Can Dance* remix album, as well as on 1990's *The Immaculate Collection*. In 2003, it was remixed as 'Into the Hollywood Groove', featuring a rap by Missy Elliott, for a Gap commercial, also appearing on that year's *Remixed & Revisited* EP courtesy of The Passengerz.

'Gambler'

Geffen Records: A 6585 **Single release:** September 1985 **Soundtrack:** *Vision Quest/Crazy for You*
Writer: Madonna
Producer: Jellybean

Madonna's other *Vision Quest* single is this oft discounted hit, never released as a single in the US. A UK Top 5 hit and Australian Top 10 single, 'Gambler' tossed its chips rather winningly between punk-dance and radio-friendly pop and at the time of its release merely added to Madonna's already bulging arsenal of hits. Only ever performed during her 1985 Virgin Tour, 'Gambler' signalled not just the near end of Madonna's working relationship with Jellybean, but the start of her new life with new husband, Sean Penn, having gotten married literally days before its release. Speaking of big gambles!

VID BIT!

Director: Harold Becker

Although the official 'Gambler' video was comprised of clips from *Vision Quest* interspersed with shots of Madonna singing the song in the movie, many territories opted for a live version from the *Madonna Live: The Virgin Tour* show from Detroit.

REMIX FIX!

Still clinging on for dear life to Madonna's toy boy belt, Jellybean added extra bells and whistles, literally, to an extended dance mix of 'Gambler'.

3

The *True Blue* Era

True Blue
Sire: 1-25442
Released: June 1986
Side A

'Papa Don't Preach'	4:27
'Open Your Heart'	4:12
'White Heat'	4:25
'Live to Tell'	5:45

Side B

'Where's the Party'	4:20
'True Blue'	4:16
'La Isla Bonita'	4:01
'Jimmy Jimmy'	3:54
'Love Makes the World Go Round'	4:27

'Live to Tell'

Sire: 9 28717-7 **Single release:** March 1986 **Album:** *True Blue*
Writers/Producers: Madonna, Patrick Leonard

After working on the Jacksons' Victory tour in 1984, Madonna brought Leonard on board as musical director/keyboardist for her 1985 Virgin Tour and from there they collaborated on her third album, *True Blue*. The album's classy and classic first single was 'Live to Tell', which *Rolling Stone* rightfully described as moody, confessional and haunting. A #1 US and #2 UK hit, it was written, according to Madonna, 'about my childhood, my mother and my stepmother' and featured in the movie *At Close Range*, starring her new husband, Sean Penn. Performed during both 1990's Blond Ambition and 2006 Confessions Tour,

'Live to Tell' was shrouded in controversy for its religious imagery, iconography, and staging. In 2020, 'LTT' was mooted as a title for Madonna's tell-all biopic.

VID BIT!

Director: James Foley

Sporting a low-key blonde look, Madonna dressed down and got remorseful, amidst scenes of Sean Penn from *At Close Range*, in this emotionally-wrenching video.

'Papa Don't Preach'

Sire: 7-28660 **Single release:** June 1986 **Album:** *True Blue*
Writers: Brian Elliot, Madonna (additional lyrics)
Producers: Madonna, Stephen Bray

The second single from *True Blue* was its biggest hit, if not biggest controversy. Composer Elliot based the lyrics on teenage girl gossip he had overheard. Madonna told *Rolling Stone*, '"Papa Don't Preach" just fit right in with my own personal zeitgeist of standing up to male authorities, whether it's The Pope, or the Catholic Church, or my father and his conservative, patriarchal ways.' Madonna sang about 'keeping my baby', but Madonna's publicist Liz Rosenberg sagely declared Madonna was 'singing a song not taking a stand'. 'Papa Don't Preach' became Madonna's first single to simultaneously top the UK and US charts. Urban legend has it the song's string opening was inspired by Madonna's love for ABBA's 1979 song 'As Good As New'. In 2002, Kelly Osbourne rockily covered Madonna's preachy classic, while in 2004, Mario Winans sampled 'Papa Don't Preach' for his 'Never Really Was' single.

VID BIT!

Director: James Foley

Back again for his second Madonna video, Foley created a timeless story around the 'Papa Don't Preach' lyrics starring the late Danny Aiello as her father, while former Studio 54 bartender Alex McArthur was her handsome *beau*. Yet the real star of the video might have been Madonna's must-have 'Italians Do It Better' T-shirt.

REMIX FIX!

Stephen Bray's Extended Version elongated the LP version by over a minute.

'Open Your Heart'

Sire: 9 28505-7 **Single release:** November 1986 **Album:** *True Blue*
Writers: Madonna, Gardner Cole, Peter Rafelson
Producers: Madonna, Patrick Leonard

The second of the two powerhouse songs brought in from other writers, 'Open Your Heart' became *True Blue's* fourth blockbuster single. Originally demoed for Cyndi Lauper as 'Follow Your Heart', as Rafelson was a big fan, it sneakily found its way to a tape of potential songs for Madonna instead. A demo with the lyrics sung by co-writer Cole's then girlfriend Donna De Lory was duly presented. 'Madonna did write a couple of lines,' Rafelson revealed about Madonna's fifth US #1 (and a UK #4), 'and got a third of the record which I was happy to give.'

VID BIT!

Director: Jean-Baptiste Mondino

After Sean Penn bowed out, French auteur Mondino was handpicked as director. While previous Madonna videos had merely hinted at sexual freedom, 'Open Your Heart' with its peep show, homoerotica, voyeurism, and strippers was her first sexually provocative work. On the video's thirty-fifth anniversary in 2021, Madonna was all heart deeming it 'still hot'.

REMIX FIX!

An Extended Version—all 10:35 minutes—courtesy of Steve Thompson & Michael Barbiero was a major party starter.

'White Heat'

Release: June 1986 **Album:** *True Blue*
Writers/Producers: Madonna, Patrick Leonard

The B-side of 1987's 'Who's That Girl' single, and one of four non-single songs from *True Blue*, had the unenviable task of following 'Papa Don't Preach' and 'Open Your Heart' as track three. With a snippet of actors James Cagney and Hank Fallon from the classic 1949 movie *White Heat* the lyrics forge a tenuous link because Madonna's 'love is dangerous, this is a bust'. With its markedly tinny 1980s production, however, 'White Heat' has cooled considerably in appeal over the years.

'Where's the Party'

Release: June 1986 **Album:** *True Blue*
Writers/Producers: Madonna, Stephen Bray, Patrick Leonard

An ecstatically hedonistic ode to weekend partying, losing control and not growing old too fast, 'Where's the Party' helped *True Blue* become the biggest selling album of the 1980s by a female artist with over 25 million copies sold.

In late 1987, Shep Pettibone's Extended Remix was promoed on 12″ vinyl with 'Spotlight', while the single version of 'Where's the Party' garnered enough airplay to appear in the US Top 40 airplay charts despite no official release. Perhaps it should have rightly been *True Blue*'s sixth single after all. In 2017, Leonard uploaded a snippet of the demo, 'Dance With Me', minus Madonna vocals, which has since disappeared. Party on, dude!

'True Blue'

Sire: 9 28591-7 **Single release:** September 1986 **Album:** *True Blue*
Writers/Producers: Madonna, Stephen Bray

In 1986, Madonna was a married lady very much in love with husband Sean Penn. Not only did she write a song about it, this one, but dedicated her album of the same name, *True Blue*, to him. With the album released in June that year and the 'True Blue' single, the album's third, following in September, it was as if nothing could spoil their cosy lovefest. Except for the movie they made together! Released between the two 'True Blues' in August, *Shanghai Surprise* was a colossal flop. Not that the world noticed much with 'True Blue' a UK #1 and a US #3.

Vid Bit!
Director: James Foley

While the rest of the world got the gooey girl group video, featuring Madonna besties Debi Mazar and Erika Belle, the US went with the winners of MTV's 'Make a Video' competition, Angel Garcia and Cliff Guests, filmed for under $1,000.

Remix Fix!

For The Color Mix of 'True Blue' Madonna was impeccably matched with the world's hottest remixer, Shep Pettibone. Peter Slaghuis, aka Hithouse, also remixed 'True Blue' for Disco Mix Club (DMC) exclusively for DJs.

'La Isla Bonita'

Sire: 9 28425-7 **Single release:** February 1987 **Album:** *True Blue*
Writers: Madonna, Patrick Leonard, Bruce Gaitsch
Producers: Madonna, Patrick Leonard

The fifth and final single from *True Blue* in 1987, 'La Isla Bonita' is Madonna's sweet, summertime Spanish lullaby. Initially submitted by Leonard and his old pal from Chicago, session guitarist Gaitsch, for Michael Jackson's *Bad* album, after their Latin jam was rejected in instrumental demo form it came to

Madonna. She rewrote the guide lyrics as a tribute to the 'beauty and mystery of Latin American people', and her enduring love affair with all things Latin. Ostensibly about a town in Belize, Madonna later confessed to *Rolling Stone*, 'I may have been on the way to the studio and seen an exit ramp for San Pedro' in LA. Another UK chart-topper, 'La Isla Bonita' reached #4 in the US, but became the biggest European hit of 1987.

Vid Bit!

Director: Mary Lambert

Filmed in early 1987 in Los Angeles (exit Hollywood!), 'La Isla Bonita' saw the welcome return of Lambert to the director's chair. With up and coming actor Benicio del Toro loitering moodily in the background, this was Madonna's languid love affair with all things Latin rapturously captured on film. With over 500 million views 'La Isla Bonita' is also Madonna's most viewed YouTube video.

Remix Fix!

The Extended Remix by Chris Lord-Alge does exactly what it says—simply extends 'La Isla Bonita' to almost five and a half minutes.

'Jimmy Jimmy'

Release: June 1986 **Album:** *True Blue*
Writers/Producers: Madonna, Stephen Bray

Another Hollywood reference via this tribute to 1950s cult hero/actor James 'Jimmy' Dean, one of Madonna's childhood idols, 'Jimmy Jimmy' is the only song from the entire *True Blue* album Madonna never got around to performing live. Once again tapping into a 1960s girl group vibe with Bray's help, Madonna's ardent love for the era burns brightly throughout. The full uncropped inlay shot of Herb Ritts' iconic *True Blue* cover exposed Madonna wearing a leather jacket in a fashionable tribute to James Dean (later namechecked in both 1990's 'Vogue' and 2015's 'Superstar').

'Love Makes the World Go Round'

Release: June 1986 **Album:** *True Blue*
Writers/Producers: Madonna, Patrick Leonard

This song had its debut a year earlier at 1985's global *Live Aid* concert. After Madonna declared, 'I ain't taking shit off today!' in response to her *Playboy* and *Penthouse* nudes being published, 'Love Makes the World Go Round' closed out the *True Blue* album in a hopeful, fully-clothed manner. The origins of 'Love Makes the World Go Round' go back to a pre-Virgin Tour party when Leonard and Madonna wrote it as their first song together. In 2021, to mark the thirty-fifth anniversary of *True Blue*, an expanded eighteen-track collection (the original nine tracks plus nine previously released mixes) hit digital platforms.

'Each Time You Break My Heart' (Nick Kamen)

WEA: 248 527-7 **Single release:** November 1986 **Album:** *Nick Kamen*
Writers/Producers: Madonna, Stephen Bray

Kamen was Madonna's British *protégé*/'toy boy', whose eponymous debut album included 'Each Time You Break My Heart', co-written and produced by Bray and Madonna and featuring Madonna on backing vocals. With a video directed by Jean-Baptiste Mondino, Kamen scored a UK #5 hit and some success in the US dance charts, thanks to Shep Pettibone's remix. Two decades later, Madonna's original lo-fi demo of 'Each Time You Break My Heart' finally leaked. Kamen, sadly, died of cancer in May 2021 aged fifty-nine.

4

The *Who's That Girl* Soundtrack/*You Can Dance* Era

Who's That Girl (Original Motion Picture Soundtrack)
Sire: 9 25611 2
Released: July 1987
Tracklist

Madonna	'Who's That Girl'	3:58
Madonna	'Causing a Commotion'	4:20
Madonna	'The Look of Love'	4:03
Duncan Faure	'24 Hours'	3:38
Club Nouveau	'Step by Step'	4:43
Michael Davidson	'Turn It Up'	3:56
Scritti Politti	'Best Thing Ever'	3:51
Madonna	'Can't Stop'	4:45
Coati Mundi	'El Coco Loco (So So Bad)'	6:22

You Can Dance
Sire: 9 25535-2
Released: November 1987
Tracklist

'Spotlight'	6:23
'Holiday' (Remix—Jellybean)	6:32
'Everybody' (Remix—Bruce Forest, Frank Heller)	6:43
'Physical Attraction'	6:20
'Over and Over' (Remix—Steve Thompson & Michael Barbiero)	7:11
'Into the Groove' (Remix—Shep Pettibone)	8:26
'Where's the Party' (Remix—Shep Pettibone)	7:16
CD extra dub versions	
'Holiday' (Dub Version)	6:56
'Into the Groove' (Dub Version)	6:23

'Where's the Party' (Dub Version)	6:20
Cassette extra dub versions	
'Into the Groove' (Dub Version)	6:23
'Over and Over' (Dub Version)	6:45

'Who's That Girl'

Sire: 7-28341 **Single release:** June 1987 **Soundtrack:** *Who's That Girl*
Writers/Producers: Madonna, Patrick Leonard

Madonna has often referred to her movie soundtrack songs as 'assignment' work and after 'Into the Groove' and 'Crazy for You', there were high hopes here. The title track, and first single, may have originally drawn some disparagement as a somewhat lesser version of 'La Isla Bonita' with its Spanish language chorus and looping, Latin beat, yet 'Who's That Girl' was another #1 in both the US and UK. As a constant media theme, and signature song, the title also came to reflect Madonna's constant reinventions.

VID BIT!

Director: Peter Rosenthal

With Chris Finch as her boy buddy (the same role he portrayed on her Who's That Girl World Tour) Madonna debuted a new hip Latina persona with darker short hair.

REMIX FIX!

Credit Steve Thompson and Michael Barbiero for Madonna's final 'clunky 80s' mixes.

'Causing a Commotion'

Sire: 9 28224-7 **Single release:** August 1987 **Soundtrack:** *Who's That Girl*
Writers/Producers: Madonna, Stephen Bray

Bray called this US #2 and UK #4 a 'party from the gate', but were the lyrics of 'Causing a Commotion' a veiled attempt by Madonna to speak directly to husband Sean Penn about 'keeping our love alive?' Penn spent a month in jail for assaulting a photographer and, just after 'Causing a Commotion' hit the charts, Madonna filed for divorce. She withdrew the papers shortly after, only to resubmit them in 1989. What a commotion!

VID BIT!

Director: Egbert van Hees

A full of commotion clip from the Who's That Girl World Tour was put in motion in most territories.

Remix Fix!

Madonna had the good sense to redial Shep Pettibone and (with a little assistance from Junior Vasquez) they finally got her into the groove of house music. Yay!

'The Look of Love'

Sire: W8115T **Single release:** November 1987 **Soundtrack:** *Who's That Girl*
Writers/Producers: Madonna, Patrick Leonard

Released outside the US as the third single from the *Who's That Girl* soundtrack, 'The Look of Love' is closely related to 'Live to Tell'. This atmospheric synth-pop ballad, a UK #9 hit (her smallest hit there for three years) was only performed live on her Who's That Girl World Tour and unjustifiably forgotten about for 1995's *Something to Remember* ballad compilation.

Vid Bit!

Director: James Foley

A compilation of clips from the *Who's That Girl* movie were used to promote the single.

'Can't Stop'

Release: July 1987 **Soundtrack:** *Who's That Girl*
Writers/Producers: Madonna, Stephen Bray

Tucked away near the end of the *Who's That Girl* soundtrack, 'Can't Stop' is a long-forgotten, by-the-numbers Madonna/Bray dance-pop nugget. As it races to its finish 'Can't Stop' suddenly gets a whole lot more exciting with Madonna and backing singers creating a major sixties girl group moment. Reviewing the *Who's That Girl* soundtrack, *Smash Hits* rightly called 'Can't Stop' 'a jaunty effort'.

'Santa Baby'

A&M Records: SP-3911 **Year:** November 1987 **Compilation:** *A Very Special Christmas*
Writers: Joan Javits, Philip Springer, Tony Springer
Producer: Jimmy Iovine

Never let it be said Madonna is a bah-humbug who does not do Christmas, here covering Eartha Kitt's 1953 naughty girl stocking stuffer 'Santa Baby'.

Produced for the Special Olympics (now the Paralympics), *A Very Special Christmas* became a perennial Yuletide seller, featuring artists like Whitney Houston, Bruce Springsteen, and Sting revisiting festive standards. With cover art designed by Madonna buddy/artist Keith Haring the album sold over 2.5 million copies.

'Spotlight'

Sire: PS-1054 **Single release:** April 1988 (Japan) **Remix Album:** *You Can Dance*
Writers: Madonna, Stephen Bray, Curtis Hudson
Producer: Stephen Bray

Spotlight signified a reunion of sorts with 'Holiday' co-writer Hudson. Inspired by the Sly & The Family Stone 1970 hit 'Everybody is a Star', 'Spotlight' did shine the spotlight on Madonna's *You Can Dance* remix compilation as its album opener. A Japanese-only single (and CD mini!), reaching #3 with a Who's That Girl World Tour collage as its video, 'Spotlight' featured in a series of commercials Madonna made for Mitsubishi. It was, however, played so much on American radio in early 1988 the song entered the lower rungs of the airplay charts despite no official release.

REMIX FIX!
An Extended Mix by Jellybean (in his final Madonna turn) was promoed to clubs.

5

The *Like a Prayer* Era

Like a Prayer
Sire: 925 844-1
Released: March 1989
Side A

'Like a Prayer'	5:39
'Express Yourself'	4:37
'Love Song'	4:52
'Till Death Us Do Part'	5:16
'Promise to Try'	3:36

Side B

'Cherish'	5:03
'Dear Jessie'	4:20
'Oh Father'	4:57
'Keep It Together'	5:03
'Spanish Eyes'	5:15
'Act of Contrition'	2:19

'Like a Prayer'

Sire: 9 27539-7 **Single release:** March 1989 **Album:** *Like a Prayer*
Writers/Producers: Madonna, Patrick Leonard

'"Like a Prayer" is a very important song to me,' Madonna once disclosed. 'I felt the impact that it was going to make … it's from my heart.' The lead single from her fourth album, also called *Like a Prayer*, was that magical, mystical, and almost mythical point where Madonna's commercial success and—finally—critical acclaim melded for the very first time. It also enabled her to reshape the definition of not just a female pop star, but any pop star. Of course, this being

Madonna, 'Like a Prayer' did not come without some controversy attached (see below). Despite this, the single raced to #1 in almost every territory it was released including the US, UK, Australia, Japan, and Canada. 'Like a Prayer' was such a big hit it is still ranked in the top 500 biggest charts hits of all time in the US. Memorably Madonna performed it at the *Live 8* benefit concert in 2005 with Ethiopian famine survivor Birhan Woldu and as her closing song at the 2012 Super Bowl halftime show. 'Like a Prayer' made history for Madonna and continues to do so over thirty years after it was first released.

VID BIT!

Director: Mary Lambert

Madonna's plan with the 'Like a Prayer' video was to make a statement on racism. Madonna had earlier filmed a two-minute commercial for Pepsi, directed by Joe Pytka called 'Make a Wish', using 'Like a Prayer'. After the premiere of the 'Like a Prayer' video, with the Vatican joining in to condemn the clip as 'blasphemy' demanding a boycott, Pepsi pulled its sweetly inoffensive Madonna ad. The proper video has since been ranked 'Most Groundbreaking Video of All Time' by MTV and second-best music video of all time by *Billboard* magazine (after Michael Jackson's 'Thriller' from 1983). Thirty-one years later, the message of the 'Like a Prayer' video was never more relevant than in the post-George Floyd BLM world. 'The Past Catches up to the future,' Madonna wrote on social media in June 2020. 'This video was made 30 years ago and caused so much controversy Because

1. I depicted police brutality and an arrest of an innocent Black Man.
2. I went to a church to pray for justice and discovered a Black Saint.
3. That Saint was crying—he had feelings.
4. I kissed that Black Saint.
5. I did my best to get him released from prison for a crime he did not commit. My contract with Pepsi was cancelled.

We all have such a long way to go but this long overdue Revolution that is happening right now in America is so great to not only witness the Change but to see all these great young leaders emerging.'

At the end of 2020, Spin.com ranked 'Like a Prayer' as the best video of the last thirty-five years calling it 'high art'.

REMIX FIX!

Though Bill Bottrell stealthily mixed in 'Act of Contrition' for his retakes, just like a prayer, Shep Pettibone took us there with his peerless dance remakes. There were so many Pettibone blessings a *Remixed Prayers* EP was later released with cover art by Madonna's brother, Christopher (also the 12″ cover). In March 2021, a digital album featuring nine 'Like a Prayer' remixes—three previously vinyl-only—was issued on Rhino.

'Act of Contrition'

Single release: March 1989 (B-side of 'Like a Prayer') **Album:** *Like a Prayer*
Writers/Producers: Madonna, Patrick Leonard ('The Powers that be')

Madonna dedicated the *Like a Prayer* album to 'my mother who taught me how to pray.' Quite what Mama Madonna (may she rest in peace) would have made of her daughter reciting the Catholic 'Act of Contrition' prayer before turning it into a rant about airline reservations will forevermore remain unknown. The B-side of the 'Like a Prayer' single is also the album's madcap closer. 'The engineer just flipped over the tape of "Like a Prayer" and played it backwards and Madonna just sat there with a microphone and said a prayer, just like that,' Leonard explained. 'The guitar on it is Prince's.' 'Act of Contrition'— which Leonard insisted was not 'intended to offend anyone, just to be fun'—is a true act of deeply dark humour. Amen.

'Express Yourself'

Sire: 9 22948-7 **Single release:** May 1989 **Album:** *Like a Prayer*
Writers/Producers: Madonna, Stephen Bray

Launched with one of Madonna's trademark energetic live performances on the 1989 *MTV Video Music Awards* (which also including a spot of voguing!) 'Express Yourself' was a first-class successor to 'Like a Prayer' as that album's follow-up single and certainly in no way 'second best'. As a single, 'Express Yourself' reached #2 in the US and #5 in Australia and the UK and its legacy is as the original 'girl power' anthem, inspiring countless other female performers such as Spice Girls, Christina Aguilera, and Lady Gaga. Gaga's 2011 single 'Born This Way' even seemed like a 'reductive' refashioning of 'Express Yourself', so Madonna cheekily incorporated it into a mash-up during her 2012 MDNA Tour, baby.

VID BIT!
Director: David Fincher

The first of four music videos Fincher directed for Madonna expressed itself with a flash of inspiration from classic 1927 silent movie *Metropolis*. Her love interest, hunky model Cameron Alborzian, went on to write books under the name of Yogi Cameron. Years later Fincher described his bond with Madonna thus: 'Madonna is my Vatican, she's my Sistine Chapel'.

REMIX FIX!
Shep Pettibone was back knob twiddling and Madonna was so enamoured of his zeitgeist talents Shep's 7″ pop-house remix became the single and video version. The original five remixes were digitally released in May 2021.

'Love Song'

Release: March 1989 **Album:** *Like a Prayer*
Writers/Producers: Madonna, Prince

Recorded at Prince's Paisley Park Studios, Madonna ventured to Minneapolis 'to write some stuff with him, but the only thing I really dug was "Love Song"'. A decidedly anti-love song (*Encyclopedia Madonnica* termed it a 'hate fuck') this at least fit *Like a Prayer*'s overall divorce manifesto. Prince's squealing guitar can be heard, like book ends, on both 'Like a Prayer' and 'Act of Contrition'.

'Till Death Do Us Part'

Release: March 1989 **Album:** *Like a Prayer*
Writers: Madonna, Patrick Leonard

With Madonna having filed for divorce from Sean Penn, again, 'Till Death Us Do Part' is literally an autobiographical account of her ill-fated marriage. Originally titled 'State of Matrimony', Madonna conceded that during the creation of the *Like a Prayer* project both she and Leonard were 'in a very dark state of mind'. While the jangly upbeat tone of 'Till Death Do Us Part' appears almost out of sync with the brutal, confessional lyrics, it is a sly match done on purpose to confound expectations about Madonna. If this was the birth of therapeutic pop, then it was also Madonna's coming of age record. In 2015, Madonna said the thing she missed the least about marriage is being 'the wife' which she called 'the worst'.

'Promise to Try'

Release: March 1989 **Album:** *Like a Prayer*
Writers: Madonna, Patrick Leonard

After tackling her husband's abuse and addiction issues, her father's anger, and her Catholic guilt on *Like a Prayer*, the only thing left—and perhaps the biggest trauma of her entire life—was that of the death of her French-Canadian mother, also called Madonna, in 1963 from breast cancer when Madonna was five years old. In just over three and a half minutes, Madonna hugs her inner 'little girl' and her voice was never before so raw and choked up with emotion as on 'Promise to Try'. Madonna's mother would have been proud of her.

'Cherish'

Sire: 9 22883-7 **Single release:** August 1989 **Album:** *Like a Prayer*
Writers/Producers: Madonna, Patrick Leonard

Was there ever a better Madonna rhyming couplet than 'Romeo and Juliet/
They never felt this way I bet?' The third single from *Like a Prayer*, deliriously
endearing 'Cherish' was initially not going to be included as Madonna thought
its cheery, upbeat tone did not match the rest of the material. Luckily, she was
convinced otherwise. The doo-wop '60s bounce of 'Cherish' peaked at #2 in
the US (kept off the top spot by Janet Jackson's 'Miss You Much') and #3 in the
UK. Madonna has only ever performed the song live on 1990's Blond Ambition
World Tour, later deriding it as 'retarded'. 'Cherish' is the word we use.

VID BIT!

Director: Herb Ritts

Filmed in Malibu and in a murky swimming pool (for the mer-men section), the
enchanting 'Cherish' video was the first ever made by Ritts, thanks to Madonna's
generous encouragement. One of the 'Cherish' mer-men was Tony Ward, later to
appear in Madonna's 'Justify My Love' video, *Sex* book, and in her bed.

REMIX FIX!

Not so much a remix, as an extended mix, courtesy of Leonard.

'Dear Jessie'

Sire: W2668T **Single release:** December 1989 **Album:** *Like a Prayer*
Writers/Producers: Madonna, Patrick Leonard

'The music was very playful and it sounded like a child and Madonna started
coming up with "pink elephants and lemonade,"' Leonard explained in 1989 about
'Dear Jessie'. 'I was saying it's got a very Beatles-like attitude, like "Dear Prudence"
and she said "Dear Jessie". Madonna and (Leonard's then three-year-old daughter)
Jessie have been friends since she was born.' As a single, Madonna's UK record
company deemed 'Dear Jessie' a suitably family friendly option for the all-important
Christmas #1 spot. In the end 'Dear Jessie', the fourth UK *like a Prayer* single in a
one-year period, peaked at #5. In many ways 'Dear Jessie' is a forerunner for 1998's
'Little Star', the ambient lullaby dedicated to daughter Lourdes.

VID BIT!

Director: Derek Hayes/Animation City

Madonna as Tinker Bell? Perhaps the cutesy 'Dear Jessie' was her audition
tape for 1991's *Hook* movie, later to star Julia Roberts in the role. In 2014,

Leonard revealed the childlike 'Dear Jessie' video animation was based on a photo of his daughter, Jessie.

'Oh Father'

Sire: 922 723-7 **Single release:** October 1989 **Album:** *Like a Prayer*
Writers/Producers: Madonna, Patrick Leonard

Written in New York when Madonna was appearing in the original Broadway production of David Mamet's *Speed-The-Plow* play, 'Oh Father' is Madonna's unqualified *magnum opus* of the 1980s, if not her entire career. This monumental, lyrically intense and spellbinding power ballad rumination on all things fatherly might have seemed like an odd choice for a single (it was *Like a Prayer*'s fourth US single), but in terms of demonstrating Madonna's artistry and commitment to her vision, 'Oh Father' is a *bona fide* career highlight. 'It was like the second half of "Live to Tell" in a way. It was the combo package,' Madonna divulged, 'it was about my father and my husband.' The 'Oh Father' single peaked at #20 in the US, not being released in other territories until 1995, when it featured on the ballads collection, *Something to Remember*, sneaking up to #16 in the UK charts. 'Oh Father' is, Leonard told *Billboard* in 2014, 'my favourite thing that we ever recorded. Ever.'

VID BIT!
Director: David Fincher

'Oh Father', through Madonna and Fincher's shared vision, became a chilling, cathartic and cinematic classic. *Rolling Stone* magazine included it among their list of the 100 Top Music Videos. 'I had kinda talked Madonna into releasing "Oh Father" as a single and the song wasn't a hit,' Fincher revealed, 'so she came back to me and said, "You screwed me up. You wanted to make this video for the song and no one liked the song and I went to bat for you and now I have to make a video by Tuesday." And I said, "What's the song called?" And she said, "Vogue."'

'Keep It Together'

Sire: 0-21427 **Single release:** January 1990 **Album:** *Like a Prayer*
Writers/Producers: Madonna, Stephen Bray

The second *Like a Prayer* Madonna/Bray co-write—which *Smash Hits* called 'the Madonna story set to music'—also became her first single of the 1990s. This ode to family love, bonds and history was the final single from *Like a Prayer* (though not released in the UK), returning Madonna to the US Top 10 after the relative chart failure of 'Oh Father'. Despite the lack of a video, Shep Pettibone's sparkling single remix of 'Keep It Together' turned a funk tribute, featuring Prince on guitar, into a club classic. Later in 1990 it would find a suitable home as the B-side to *Vogue* in Europe, while in Australia 'Keep It Together' was a joint #1 double A-side. 'Keep It Together' also marked Bray's final work with Madonna. In 1997, he released *Pre-Madonna*, a collection of ten Madonna demo recordings (see entry in Appendix I) and in 2006 was nominated for a Tony.

REMIX FIX!

'Keep It Together' was, of course, supposed to be the single where a certain dance tune Shep Pettibone and Madonna breezily knocked off about the passing voguing craze would be its B-side. That plan axed, Pettibone sprinkled his house magic dust on 'Keep It Together', while DJ Mark 'the 45 King' and Stephen Bray reproduced a mix giving more space to Prince's guitar playing chops.

'Spanish Eyes'

Release: March 1989 **Album:** *Like a Prayer*
Writers/Producers: Madonna, Patrick Leonard

As was now customary, every Madonna album had to have one Latin-influenced track and with a title like 'Spanish Eyes' (retitled 'Pray for Spanish Eyes' on some editions) there was no disguising that here. Tucked away near the end of side two of the *Like a Prayer* album is this mournful ballad which *Smash Hits* called 'like a slow Part Two to "La Isla Bonita"'. Initial pressings of the *Like a Prayer* album, incidentally, came with a guide to safe sex card tucked inside the album sleeve, which smelled of patchouli to invoke church incense. Like wonder *Rolling Stone* magazine called *Like a Prayer* 'as close to art as pop music gets' as it sold over 15 million copies.

'Supernatural'

Single release: August 1989 (B-side to 'Cherish') **Compilation:** *Red Hot + Dance*
Writers/Producers: Madonna, Patrick Leonard

'It's almost a novelty piece,' Leonard told *Smash Hits* in 1989 about 'Supernatural'. 'The lyrics are about sleeping with someone who's dead in a spiritual sense. It's about sleeping with a ghost. It's a real kind of weird funk tune with a very strange groove.' For fans who missed this ghoulish outing on the B-side for 'Cherish', Madonna later donated 'Supernatural' to 1992's *Red Hot + Dance* AIDS charity album remixed by Sly & Robbie. The iconic *Red Hot + Dance* album cover was taken from an artwork by Madonna's former bestie, Keith Haring.

'Angels with Dirty Faces'

Uploaded to YouTube: July, 2019
Writers/Producers: Madonna, Patrick Leonard

Thirty years after the release of the *Like a Prayer* album, Leonard uploaded this demo from those 1988 sessions to stop it being auctioned off. It is easy to see why the mid-tempo 'Angels with Dirty Faces' did not make the final cut, sounding like a few steps backwards to the *Who's That Girl* era. While much has been made over the years about Madonna's ability to be a trend spotter and work with the right people at the right time, her other angelic gift is knowing which songs to retain and which to discard.

6

The *I'm Breathless* Era

I'm Breathless: Music from and inspired by the film Dick Tracy
Sire: 9 26209-2
Released: May 1990
Tracklist

'He's a Man'	4:42
'Sooner or Later'	3:18
'Hanky Panky'	3:57
'I'm Going Bananas'	1:41
'Cry Baby'	4:04
'Something to Remember'	5:03
'Back in Business'	5:10
'More'	4:56
'What Can You Lose'	2:08
'Now I'm Following You (Part I)'	1:35
'Now I'm Following You (Part II)'	3:18
'Vogue'	4:50

'Vogue'

Sire: 0-21513 **Single release:** March 1990 **Soundtrack:** *I'm Breathless*
Writers/Producers: Madonna, Shep Pettibone
   'What are you looking at?!' Originally intended as the B-side for the 'Keep It Together' single and recorded for just $5,000, *Vogue* is now considered Madonna's signature song. Named after voguing, a style of dancing popular in NYC's black and Latin gay ballroom scene at the time, 'Vogue' adroitly and glossily blended house music with disco. Pettibone and then silent partner Tony Shimkin recycled their remix of Janet Jackson's 1989 'Miss You Much' hit for

its foundations, while Madonna struck a pose with a celebrated spoken word section namechecking stars from the golden age of Hollywood. When 'Vogue' was first recorded and presented to her record label they far-sightedly realized it should be a standalone single, if not the selling point for her upcoming *I'm Breathless* soundtrack promoting the *Dick Tracy* movie she was starring in. The biggest selling single of 1990—2 million copies in the US alone—'Vogue' is also Madonna's biggest selling single. Musically it is unmistakably inspired by 1982's soul-disco 'Ooh I Love It (Love Break)' by Salsoul Orchestra who, via Tony Shimkin and Curt Fresca (both worked on 'Vogue'), sued Pettibone/Madonna in 2013 for sampling a track Pettibone had essentially recreated but lost the lawsuit. *Time* magazine named 'Vogue' 'the most famous fashion song of all time', it has been inducted into the Rock and Roll Hall of Fame, and it also served as the musical starting point for the second series of Ryan Murphy's hit TV series *Pose*, set in 1990. Celebrating thirty years since it topped the US charts, *Billboard* defined 'Vogue' as 'a magical, life's-a-ball moment of transcendence few dance songs dare to reach', just as Lady Gaga's strutting 'Babylon' from 2020's *Chromatica* album paid clear homage to 'Vogue'. Later that year *Inside the Groove* podcast conclusively identified 'Vogue' having brazenly sampled two earlier Madonna classics—'Lucky Star' and 'Like a Virgin'.

VID BIT!

Director: David Fincher

Filmed in saturated B&W, taking inspiration from the art deco movement, the paintings of Tamara de Lempicka and photographs of Horst, this is when Madonna brought voguing to the masses, thanks to her dancers who would accompany her on that year's Blond Ambition World Tour. 'Vogue' additionally, fashionistas, featured the debut of her legendary 'cone bra'. Considered one of the greatest, if not the greatest music video of all time, Fincher revealed the 'Vogue' video was shot in just sixteen hours before Madonna started her tour. Essential viewing is also required of Madonna's riveting 'Dangerous Liaisons' performance of 'Vogue' at 1990's *MTV Video Music Awards*.

REMIX FIX!

Pettibone served all the 'Vogue' remixes, with none straying far from his go with the flow, bump'n'grind original. FYI: Honey Dijon spins a fierce old skool house remix in her sets.

'He's a Man'

Release: May 1990 **Soundtrack:** *I'm Breathless*
Writers/Producers: Madonna, Patrick Leonard

Peculiarly, Madonna's follow-up album to *Like a Prayer* is not considered her next 'studio' album. Instead, *I'm Breathless: Music from and inspired by the film Dick Tracy* is deemed a soundtrack outing. It is so much more than that, although its first track, 'He's a Man', was neither a big band era ballad, nor a swinging *entrée* to a movie set in the 1930s. Perhaps the best thing about 'He's a Man' is the backing trio of Madonna staples Niki Haris and Donna De Lory, joined by N'Dea Davenport, soon after to find success with acid jazz purveyors Brand New Heavies.

'Sooner or Later'

Release: May 1990 **Soundtrack:** *I'm Breathless*
Writer: Stephen Sondheim
Producers: Madonna, Bill Bottrell
The first of three songs Broadway legend Sondheim wrote for his pal Warren Beatty's *Dick Tracy* movie, the clever wordplay of 'Sooner or Later' is classic Sondheim. Crooned coyly during 1990's Blond Ambition World Tour, the following year Madonna performed 'Sooner or Later' in dazzling Marilyn Monroe style at the Oscars winning Best Original Song, Sondheim's sole Academy Award. On its thirtieth anniversary, Madonna posted footage of herself performing at the Oscars with the caption: 'Singing the song "Sooner or Later" at the Academy Awards was one of the highlights of my career—not to mention my date Michael Jackson!'

'Hanky Panky'

Sire: 9 21577-0 **Single release:** June 1990 **Soundtrack:** *I'm Breathless*
Writers/Producers: Madonna, Stephen Bray
Any Madonna single that came after *Vogue* was going to endure a punishing time, but with *risqué* lines like 'tie my hands behind my back and I'm in ecstasy', or 'my bottom hurts just thinking about it', 'Hanky Panky' is a tribute to how big Madonna was at this point that she got away with it. Madonna even managed to spank her big band 'Hanky Panky' to #2 in the UK and #10 in the US, despite some radio stations blacklisting it due to its smart-assed lyrical content.

Vɪᴅ Bɪᴛ!
Director: Alek Keshishian
Madonna's on tour, but no problem, as a clip of her happy-slapping 'Hanky Panky' live during the Blond Ambition World Tour was serviced, revelling in its spanky friskiness.

REMIX FIX!
Kevin M. Gilbert's Bare Bones Single and Bare Bottom 12″ Mix were frankly bottom feeders.

'I'm Going Bananas'

Release: May 1990 **Soundtrack:** *I'm Breathless*
Writers: Michael Kernan, Andy Paley
Producers: Madonna, Patrick Leonard

¡*Hola!* Here is the *I'm Breathless* album's *loco* Latino moment—a hot tropical salsa explosion of unbridled 'booga wooga' all over before it burns past two minutes. *I'm Going Bananas* is a nod to 1930–50s 'Brazilian bombshell' Carmen Miranda and co-written by Andy Paley, who also produced that year's *Dick Tracy* soundtrack. 'I'm Going Bananas' was memorably and wackily performed during 1993's The Girlie Show tour together with *La Isla Bonita*.

'Cry Baby'

Release: May 1990 **Soundtrack:** *I'm Breathless*
Writers/Producers: Madonna, Patrick Leonard

'Cry Baby' slyly suggests Madonna and Leonard were trying their best to ape, if not emulate, a Sondheim song of their own. Did they manage it? Well, Madonna sure does deliver a keen Betty Boop vocal, the lyrics are suitably era-conscious ('My guy is such a wet noodle/He acts like a real cock-a-a-doodle') and the vibrant backing vocals make this worthy of a second listen. In *Vanity Fair* that year a modest Madonna insisted that as good as Sondheim's *Dick Tracy* songs were, hers were 'the real shit'.

'Something to Remember'

Release: May 1990 **Soundtrack:** *I'm Breathless*
Writers/Producers: Madonna, Patrick Leonard

For a few years, it seemed as if 'Something to Remember' might end up as the great forgotten Madonna ballad—assumed by many to be either about her break up with Sean Penn, or a tribute to her dance mentor Christopher Flynn who died of AIDS in 1990—though it equally fits memorably into the *Dick Tracy* movie narrative. Hidden away on *I'm Breathless*, which sold a respectable 7 million copies, it was—hurrah—resurrected in 1995 for Madonna's ballad compilation, also called *Something to Remember*, selling over 10 million copies.

'Back in Business'

Release: May 1990 **Soundtrack:** *I'm Breathless*
Writers/Producers: Madonna, Patrick Leonard

A somewhat underrated Madonna album track, 'Back in Business' features some of Madonna's slinkiest vocals, not to mention more naughtiness lyrically about 'the brighter side of living in sin'. Sondheim also wrote a song called 'Back in Business' for *Dick Tracy* because Madonna's was not considered good enough. Sondheim finished the new 'Back in Business', to be used in an action sequence, just one month before screenings of *Dick Tracy*. It was sung by Janis Siegel, a vocalist with pop/jazz combo The Manhattan Transfer. Little wonder the on-set Beatty-Ciccone romance was soon out of business.

'More'

Release: May 1990 **Soundtrack:** *I'm Breathless*
Writer: Stephen Sondheim
Producers: Madonna, Bill Bottrell

There cannot be too many pop stars who have had not one but three Sondheim songs written exclusively for them. Trademark Sondheim and a cross between a Broadway showstopper and a Weimar cabaret, 'More' is literally Sondheim's theatrical take on 'Material Girl' ('Got my diamonds, got my yacht/Got a guy I adore/I'm so happy with what I got/I want more'). 'More' features in *Dick Tracy* in both a rehearsal scene with Al Pacino as Big Boy Caprice (winning an Oscar for Best Makeup), as well as a show tune at the bustling Caprice's Club Ritz.

'What Can You Lose?'

Release: May 1990 **Soundtrack:** *I'm Breathless*
Writer: Stephen Sondheim
Producers: Madonna, Bill Bottrell

The third of the Sondheim trilogy for Madonna is this twinkly ballad featuring her *Dick Tracy* co-star and Sondheim specialist Mandy Patinkin singing lead before Madonna joins him. Warren Beatty was keen to make a *Dick Tracy* sequel but it would have been without Madonna whose character Breathless Mahoney—spoiler alert!—dies in the original. 'What Can You Lose' has been covered many times since, perhaps the best being by Tony legend Audra McDonald.Sondheim passed away in 2021, aged ninety-one.

'Now I'm Following You Part I/II'

Release: May 1990 **Soundtrack:** *I'm Breathless*
Writers: Andy Paley, Jeff Lass, Ned Claflin, Jonathan Paley
Producers: Madonna, Patrick Leonard, Kevin Gilbert

Dating Madonna during this era, she cajoled not-so-boy-toy Warren Beatty into lending his voice to this track on *I'm Breathless*. Beatty acquits himself rather well on what is a close relative to Irving Berlin's classic 'Puttin' on the Ritz'. On 'Part II', Madonna scratches the track ahead into something more dance minded, though there is a plodding '80s quality to it. Warner had vague plans post-'Vogue' to release this as a single, with a stodgy '80s dance remix commissioned from Tiny Little Circles, which leaked years later. Madonna only ever performed 'Now I'm Following You' on her Blond Ambition World Tour as a dance interlude with her favourite Dick. Tracy, that is.

7

The *Immaculate Collection* Era

The Immaculate Collection
Sire: 9 26440-2
Released: November 1990
Tracklist

'Holiday'	4:05
'Lucky Star'	3:37
'Borderline'	4:00
'Like a Virgin'	3:11
'Material Girl'	3:53
'Crazy for You'	3:45
'Into the Groove'	4:09
'Live to Tell'	5:18
'Papa Don't Preach'	4:09
'Open Your Heart'	3:51
'La Isla Bonita'	3:47
'Like a Prayer'	5:51
'Express Yourself'	4:04
'Cherish'	3:52
'Vogue'	5:18
'Justify My Love'	5:00
'Rescue Me'	5:32

'Justify My Love'

Sire: 0-21820 **Single release:** November 1990 **Compilation:** *The Immaculate Collection*
Writers: Madonna, Lenny Kravitz, Ingrid Chavez
Producers: Lenny Kravitz, André Betts

Daringly different, titillatingly racy, and undoubtedly the sexiest record Madonna, if indeed anyone, has ever recorded, 'Justify My Love' became a sensational #1 record around the world, spawned a banned video and set the scene for what was to come two years later with her *Sex* book and *Erotica* album. The key new track from her *Immaculate Collection* compilation connected her not only with Lenny Kravitz, but also his producer Betts, who would co-produce a number of tracks on 1992's *Erotica*. Lyrically the song was for the most part written by Kravitz's then secret lover Chavez, a former Prince *protégé*, who initially forewent a credit as Kravitz was at the time still married to Lisa Bonet. Chavez sued to receive due credit when the romance became public. Controversy also centred on Kravitz sampling without consent Public Enemy's 'Security of the First World', itself sampling James Brown's 'Funky Drummer' from 1970. All this and we have not even gotten to that video yet. 'Justify My Love' remains a true yearning, burning benchmark in Madonna's career. Kravitz revealed in 2020 he played the 'JML' demo for Madonna only twice before they recorded it the following day, describing the studio atmosphere as 'fun and very sensual—just know that it was all very authentic'. Chavez released her own unjustifiably lacklustre recording of 'JML' in 2020 to celebrate its thirtieth anniversary.

Vid Bit!
Director: Jean-Baptiste Mondino

'The whole idea was to lock ourselves into this hotel for three days and two nights,' Mondino reminisced, 'without any rules.' In 1990 gender fluidity, sexual exploration, and an unapologetic female pop star in the thick of it all was the stuff of headline news. MTV banned the 'Justify My Love' video—based on cult Italian film *The Night Porter*—so Madonna released 'Justify My Love' as a VHS video single, becoming the highest-selling such format ever. In 2020, Spin.com justifiably ranked 'Justify My Love' #20 on their list of best videos of the last thirty-five years.

Remix Fix!
'Justify My Love' signified the first time William Orbit and Madonna came together on record. His Orbit 12″ Mix was eerie, weird and suitably depraved, though less so compared to The Beast Within Remix, remixed by Kravitz, where Madonna recited biblical verses about Jews, wildly open to misinterpretation.

'Rescue Me'

Sire: 0-21813 **Single release:** February 1991 **Compilation:** *The Immaculate Collection*
Writers/Producers: Madonna, Shep Pettibone

Madonna at her most soulful, this growling deep house successor to 'Vogue' was one of the two new tracks on her *Immaculate Collection* greatest hits. After strong radio airplay in the US 'Rescue Me' was finally released in early 1991 as a single. Despite the lack of a video 'Rescue Me' achieved impressive Top 10 placings in both the US and UK. *The Immaculate Collection* sold over 30 million copies—the best-selling compilation by a solo artist of all time. 'Rescue Me' finally got a welcome nod from Madonna as a dance interlude (retitled 'Breathwork') during her *Madame X* 2019–2020 concerts.

VID BIT!
A cheap and cheerless corporate clip for 'Rescue Me', incongruously featuring footage of her 1987 Who's That Girl World Tour, was serviced in some territories.

REMIX FIX!
Pettibone, as Madonna's then in-house remixer, handled all remix duties. Immaculately too.

8

The *Erotica* Era

Erotica
Maverick: 9 45031-2
Released: October 1992
Tracklist

'Erotica'	5:19
'Fever'	5:00
'Bye Bye Baby'	3:56
'Deeper and Deeper'	5:33
'Where Life Begins'	5:57
'Bad Girl'	5:23
'Waiting'	5:46
'Thief of Hearts'	4:51
'Words'	5:56
'Rain'	5:24
'Why's It So Hard'	5:23
'In This Life'	6:23
'Did You Do It?'	4:54
'Secret Garden'	5:32

'Get Over' (Nick Scotti)

Reprise Records: 0-40711 **Single release:** March 1991 **Soundtrack:** *Nothing But Trouble* **Album:** *Nick Scotti*
Writers: Madonna, Stephen Bray
Producers: Madonna, Shep Pettibone

Scotti was an *über*-handsome US actor/model who managed two minor hits in 1993, one being 'Get Over'. Originally written by Madonna and Bray as a possible third new track for 1990's *Immaculate Collection*, 'Get Over' (originally titled 'Can't Get Over You') was eventually passed to Scotti, with Pettibone producing/remixing and Madonna adding her recognisable backing vocals. Although 'Get Over' was included on his self-titled debut album, it had earlier appeared on the soundtrack for the 1991 movie *Nothing But Trouble*. Madonna's original demo of 'Get Over' remains unleaked.

'This Used to be My Playground'

Sire: 7-18822 **Single release:** June 1992 **Compilation:** *Barcelona Gold*
Writers/Producers: Madonna, Shep Pettibone

Although one of the last songs recorded during the *Erotica* sessions this dreamy, pining ballad was the first to be released. 'This Used to be My Playground' was used in the female baseball movie *A League of their Own*, starring Tom Hanks, Geena Davis and Madonna typecast as 'All the Way Mae' and heard over the end credits, albeit in an extended version denied an official release. 'TUTBMP' hit #1 in the US, becoming her tenth #1 and pushing her ahead of Whitney Houston as the female with the most #1s. After receiving a Golden Globe nomination for Best Original Song, almost thirty years later Amazon produced an *A League of their Own* TV series.

VID BIT!
Director: Alek Keshishian

Previously director of Madonna's documentary *In Bed with Madonna/Truth or Dare*, as well as later co-writing her directorial effort *W.E.*, Keshishian meshed Madonna with sequences from the movie in a nostalgic photobook style. Sniffle.

'Erotica'

Maverick: 9 18782-2 **Single release:** September 1992 **Album:** *Erotica*
Writers: Madonna, Shep Pettibone, Tony Shimkin
Producers: Madonna, Shep Pettibone

Give it up, do as she says! With something to offend even the most discerning of tastes, *Erotica* was next level Madonna sexual discovery, envelope pushing and aural enhancement. 'Erotica' as a song—not just the namesake album it came from—was as if her two previous singles, 'Justify My Love' and 'Rescue Me', had buggered off on a dirty weekend together. Pettibone beefed *Erotica* up with a sample of Kool & The Gang's 1973 funk hit 'Jungle Boogie' to add, as he put it, 'a dark mysterious vibe'. Amid the swift and vicious anti-*Sex* book melee, 'Erotica'—Madonna's first release on her own record label imprint,

Maverick, which continued until 2008—got swallowed up (literally) even as it peaked at #3 in both the US and UK. In 1993 Lebanese singer Fairuz sued Madonna for sampling her 1962 Easter chant 'El Yom Ulliqa Ala Khashaba' for 'Erotica'. The case was settled out of court for $2.5 million and the *Erotica* album subsequently banned in Lebanon.

VID BIT!

Director: Fabien Baron

The 'Erotica' video is essentially furtive filthy outtakes and snoopy sleazy sequences from Madonna's *Sex* book (spot the celeb cameos!). MTV quickly banned 'Erotica' with an edited version exposing itself on 2009's *Celebration: The Video Collection*.

REMIX FIX!

Masters at Work and William Orbit were brought in, though curiously Pettibone was dismissed from remixing his own track. MAW's House Instrumental of 'Erotica' is a truly sex-citing underground gay classic.

SEX-TRA!

Copies of Madonna's *Sex* book came with a CD featuring an earlier version of 'Erotica', labelled as 'Erotic', beginning with Madonna clearing her throat. Ahem.

'Fever'

Maverick: 5439-18534-7 **Single release:** March 1993 **Album:** *Erotica*
Writers: John Davenort, Eddie Cooley
Producers: Madonna, Shep Pettibone

Sometimes the best ideas start out as happy accidents and so it was with 'Fever'. Originally Madonna was recording the track 'Goodbye to Innocence' (eventually left off *Erotica*) when she started to improvise the lyrics to Peggy Lee's sultry signature song from the late 1950s. Not issued as a single in the US, Madonna's 'Fever' hit #6 in the UK and is remarkable as one of the few covers Madonna has recorded and released.

VID BIT!

Director: Stéphane Sednaoui

Photojournalist, filmmaker and boyfriend of both Björk and later Kylie Minogue, Sednaoui filmed Madonna in her new hometown of Miami in a variety of wigs, outfits and icon guises for 'Fever'.

REMIX FIX!

Mix duties were divided up between Murk Boys (taking it Deep South and to Miami) and Pettibone adding some clubby and dubby flavours 'til it sizzles. The fizzy, unreleased 'Fever' video mix was by Daniel Abraham. Thirteen 'Fever' mixes were due to be issued as a Rhino digital album in 2021 then postponed.

'Bye Bye Baby'

Maverick: 9362-41196-2 **Single release:** November 1993 **Album:** *Erotica*
Writers: Madonna, Shep Pettibone, Tony Shimkin
Producers: Madonna, Shep Pettibone

Premiered at the *MTV Music Video Awards* in 1993 as a taster of her then upcoming The Girlie Show tour, reinventing herself as a 1930s Marlene Dietrich androgynous creature, complete with top hat, tails and cane, 'Bye Bye Baby' was the sixth and final single from the *Erotica* era. 'Bye Bye Baby' was only released as a single in a handful of territories, peaking at #15 while Madonna was in Australia for her first ever down under tour. Was it also Madonna's not-so-fond way of bidding farewell to boyfriend Tony Ward? 'I guess this song is the equivalent of breaking up with someone by text today,' Shimkin noted in 2017.

REMIX FIX!

With no video commissioned, 'Bye Bye Baby' was reliant on a set of unexceptional remixes from Ricky Crespo, part of the C+C Music Factory and Clivillés/Cole family.

'Deeper and Deeper'

Maverick: 0-40722 **Single release:** November 1992 **Album:** *Erotica*
Writers: Madonna, Tony Shimkin, Shep Pettibone
Producers: Madonna, Shep Pettibone

Written by a self-confessed fag hag and a (then) gay couple, 'Deeper and Deeper' is one of the deeply unheralded classics of queer liberation from the Madonna back catalogue. Shimkin, also reportedly Pettibone's boyfriend, called it 'a big nod to her beginnings as an artist', though it suffered at the time of release from the backlash hurled at her *Sex* book. As *Erotica*'s second single, 'Deeper and Deeper' still managed a Top 10 placing in the US and UK, topped the dance charts and was certified gold in Australia. Madonna insisted Pettibone insert a flamenco guitar instrumental break in the middle. 'I didn't like the idea of taking a Philly house song and putting "La Isla Bonita" in the middle of it,' Pettibone complained, 'but that's what she wanted, so that's what she got!' With lyrics opaquely referencing a coming out of sorts it's one of the *Erotica* album's finest moments.

Vid Bit!

Director: Bobby Woods

Oddball, eccentric and arty, this take on an indie flick *à la* Andy Warhol's Factory days, featured an appearance from future movie director Sofia Coppola. Other cameos included actor Udo Kier, Warhol actor Holly Woodlawn, gay porn director Chi Chi LaRue, gay porn star Joey Stefano (also featured in her *Sex* book), pals Debi Mazar and Ingrid Casares, future manager Guy Oseary and record label boss Seymour Stein. Director Woods was executive producer of Madonna's Boy Toy Inc. business.

Remix Fix!

Pettibone handled most of the mixes here and deeply excelled himself. David Morales was also brought in to dispense a shiny deep house polish.

'Where Life Begins'

Release: October 1992 **Album:** *Erotica*
Writers/Producers: Madonna, André Betts

While much has been made of the Madonna/Pettibone collaborations on *Erotica*, four cuts with Lenny Kravitz associate Betts were also part of the package. If anything, they signalled where Madonna would stop off next after she had laid Dita down to rest, or at least put her in a trance. 'Where Life Begins', a bumbling, freeform R&B jam was very in keeping with the 'Justify My Love' track Betts co-produced with Lenny Kravitz. 'Shep and Dré come from two different worlds,' Madonna told *Vogue* magazine that year. 'Dré has more of a street vibe, a jazz influence and hip-hop. Shep's more commercial, dance oriented.' Lyrically a not-so-coy ode to the joys of cunnilingus ('every girl should experience eating out') 'Where Love Lives' certainly at least fitted into the broader *Erotica* remit.

'Bad Girl'

Maverick: 9 40793-2 **Single release:** February 1993 **Album:** *Erotica*
Writers: Madonna, Shep Pettibone, Tony Shimkin
Producers: Madonna, Shep Pettibone

One of Madonna's most underappreciated ballads, 'Bad Girl' grinds all of the sexy talk elsewhere on the *Erotica* album to a deadly halt. Shimkin said years later he 'didn't realise how emotional 'Bad Girl' was for her until we were done with the record.' The sole, sobering live rendition of 'Bad Girl' came in 1993 on the *Saturday Night Live* TV show. In 2020 Idolator.com reassessed 'Bad Girl' as 'one of The Queen's most underrated anthems'.

Vɪᴅ Bɪᴛ!

Director: David Fincher

Released a month after her flaccid erotic thriller *Body of Evidence*, the 'Bad Girl' video was like a much more condensed, better acted and better sound-tracked version of Madonna's fourth feature film, albeit with Christopher Walken as her guardian angel (he should be sacked).

Rᴇᴍɪx Fɪx!

The original 5:23 'Bad Girl' added an extra minute or so for an Extended Mix.

'Waiting'

Release: October 1992 **Album:** *Erotica*
Writers/Producers: Madonna, André Betts

While much of the Pettibone tracks on *Erotica* were aimed at being 'the next "Vogue"', the Betts tracks seemed focused on unearthing 'the next "Justify My Love"'. In fact, according to Betts, on 'Waiting', 'I actually sampled stuff from "Justify My Love" ... the "waiting" part is actually Madonna's vocals from "Justify My Love". That was an easy sell to Madonna.' A hip-hop remix of 'Waiting', brandishing a rap by Everlast ('I can get explicit/Baby let me kiss it') and produced by Danny Saber, later appeared on the 'Rain' single.

'Thief of Hearts'

Release: October 1992 **Album:** *Erotica*
Writers: Madonna, Shep Pettibone, Tony Shimkin
Producers: Madonna, Shep Pettibone

Amid the crunch of crashing glass Madonna fist pounds her way through a booming Pettibone pop-house production as sprightly as Madonna's lyrics are unhinged. Did Madonna compose 'Thief Of Hearts' about Sean Penn's new partner Robin Wright—'Little miss thinks she can have his child/Well anybody can do it?' Considering Penn/Wright's first child, Dylan, was born in 1991, this may have been foremost in Madonna's mind writing the knife-twisting lyrics. Equally it could be directed at Warren Beatty whose first child, Kathlyn, was born in 1992 to wife Annette Bening and who in later years transitioned into transgender activist/artist Stephen Beatty. In 2021, a 'Thief of Hearts' demo emerged with early heartless lyrics including 'If I had a hammer/I'd bash your fucking head/I'd claw your fucking eyes out/All over the land'. Ouch.

'Words'

Release: October 1992 **Album:** *Erotica*
Writers: Madonna, Shep Pettibone, Tony Shimkin
Producers: Madonna, Shep Pettibone

Madonna was ahead of her time here calling out what pre-internet were called critics and nowadays are trolls. As a protest against the things written about her ('They always attack, please take them all back/if they're yours I don't want them anymore'), Madonna's danceable rant goes on the offensive against the 'smart, chic and shrewd'. Towards the end of 'Words' during a spoken word section she defines what those words actually are ('Language that is used in anger/Personal feelings signalling danger'). Word up!

'Rain'

Maverick: 9 18505-2 **Single release:** August 1993 **Album:** *Erotica*
Writers/Producers: Madonna, Shep Pettibone

Pettibone wrote 'Rain' the night before Madonna came into the studio—'it was a Sunday, it was raining—ha!' he laughed. 'Rain' was the *Erotica* album's fourth single, released in the summer of 1993 inching up to #14 on the US charts. It stalled at #7 in the UK, again a victim of the *Sex* backlash. Originally planned for a later abandoned musical adaptation of *Wuthering Heights* with her pal Alek Keshishian, 'Rain' was a highlight of 1993's The Girlie Show tour, sung by Madonna with backing besties Niki Haris and Donna De Lory. In 2016, Niki and Donna, long since finished their working relationship with Madonna, released a bittersweet electro-pop cover of 'Rain'. In 2020, it was noted Madonna released 'Rain' aged thirty-four and Lady Gaga released her 'Rain On Me' also aged thirty-four.

VID BIT!
Director: Mark Romanek

Madonna goes futuristic Japanese in a video shot in California, but made to look like Tokyo. 'Rain' featured actor/composer Ryuichi Sakamoto, who Romanek called 'the most iconic and famous and attractive Japanese icon'.

REMIX FIX!
'Rain' tapped a drippy, wet '90s Radio Remix for its single release by Daniel Abraham.

'Why's It So Hard'

Release: October 1992 **Album:** *Erotica*
Writers: Madonna, Shep Pettibone, Tony Shimkin
Producers: Madonna, Shep Pettibone

Shimkin, then Pettibone's collaborator, PA, and boyfriend at the time, and responsible for co-writing the bulk of the album, reported that halfway through *Erotica* everyone went off on vacation. 'Shep happened to go to Jamaica and I happened to go scuba diving in the Cayman Islands, and both places are heavily reggae-based culture,' Shimkin revealed. 'That's what we came back having listened to, so we decided out of nowhere to do a reggae track.' Those are also Shimkin's backing vocals on this track where Madonna goes all Earth Mother as she tries to remind us to 'love one another, love your sister, love your brother'.

'In This Life'

Release: October 1992 **Album:** *Erotica*
Writers/Producers: Madonna, Shep Pettibone

Confounding expectations, here is Madonna's moving tribute to the two gay men in her life she loved most of all—NYC bestie Martin Burgoyne and dance teacher Christopher Flynn. Both died of AIDS. Pettibone asserted in 2017 it was his idea to write a song for Burgoyne and at first Madonna was not sure it would work 'but she quickly came up with the words in about 15 minutes and that became "In This Life"'. Only ever sung live by Madonna during 1993's The Girlie Show tour, she introduced 'In This Life' during the *Live Down Under* broadcast calling it 'a song I wrote about two very dear friends of mine who died of AIDS … the greatest tragedy of the 20th century … for all of you out those who understand what I'm talking about—don't give up' before raising her fist defiantly.

'Did You Do It?'

Release: October 1992 **Album:** *Erotica*
Writers/Producers: Madonna, André Betts

Essentially 'Waiting' but with a rap and Madonna moaning. Betts admitted he did it as a joke when Madonna left the studio to go 'off for dinner with the *Sex* book guys'. He is the song's main rapper, freestyling no less, while his buddies Mark Goodman and Dave Murphy are the 'Did you do it?' guys. 'Madonna and I used to talk a lot of shit to each other,' he told *Billboard*. 'The guys used to ask me, "Did you do it? Did you have sex with her?" I'm like, "Hellllll no." And they're like, "You're lying!"' Madonna was so impressed with Betts' off-the-cuff rap she slapped it on her album.

'Secret Garden'

Release: October 1992 **Album:** *Erotica*
Writers/Producers: Madonna, André Betts

A lush ode to Madonna's lady garden, the jazzy hip-hop inflected 'Secret Garden' and closing *Erotica* track, is an oft neglected highlight, something Madonna wholeheartedly agrees with. Asked in 1994 about her greatest career regret she irately replied, 'the fact my *Erotica* album was overlooked because of the whole thing with the *Sex* book. It just got lost in all that. I think there's some brilliant songs on it and people didn't give it a chance.' The seductive leaked demo version is further proof Madonna's 'Secret Garden' is definitely worth a longer linger, while in 2020 *Slant* magazine ranked it her #1 'greatest deep cut'.

'Up Down Suite'

Single release: August 1993 (B-side to 'Rain')
Writers: Madonna, Shep Pettibone, Tony Shimkin
Producers: Madonna, Shep Pettibone

A twelve-minute dub version of 'Goodbye to Innocence' released on the B-side to the 'Rain' single is a typically unremitting Pettibone disco-house beat with some funky trumpet blasts. 'Up Down Suite' is perfect though, as one YouTuber pointed out, for having sex to, especially with Madonna chanting 'up, down' before enjoying a wailing orgasm. 'Up Down Suite' also qualifies as Madonna's longest song. There is truth in the statement though that size is not everything.

'Queen's English' (Jose & Luis)

Sire: 0-40543 **Single release:** September 1993 **Compilation:** *New Faces*
Writers: Junior Vasquez, Jose Guiterez, Luis Gamacho, M. Depeyer
Producer: Junior Vasquez

Credited to Jose & Luis, two of Madonna's *Blond Ambition* dancers, '"Queen's English" is another term for our "gay pig Latin" that we used to speak,' Luis explained. Sadly, this 'Vogue'-lite project fell over because having two openly queer pop stars was simply twenty-five years ahead of its time. Jose and Luis would reappear in 2016's *Strike a Pose* documentary examining the *Blond Ambition* dancers twenty-five years later. Jose Guiterez (Xtravaganza) became a regular on the *Pose* TV series based around the NYC vogueing/ballroom scene. 'Nobody wanted to give us a face and she did,' he reminisced to *Interview* magazine in 2021. 'I will be forever grateful'.

Vɪᴅ Bɪᴛ!
There is a poor-quality, unapologetically queer video (director unknown) featuring all manner of queens, though minus Queen Madonna.

Rᴇᴍɪx Fɪx!
Search out Mo Mo's In the House Mix where there's more Madonna than J&L.

'Goodbye to Innocence'

Sire: 9 45645-2 **Release:** July 1994 **Compilation:** *Just Say Roe Volume VII: Just Say Roe*

Writers/Producers: Madonna, Shep Pettibone

'Goodbye to Innocence' turned into a cover of Peggy Lee's 'Fever' before being resurrected for a good cause. Hidden away on pro-choice compilation, *Just Say Roe (Vol. VII Of Just Say Yes),* are its lyrics a not-so-veiled attack on stardom: 'My life is not a game that I play to entertain you/And if you can do it better/Then you're welcome to my fame'? Pettibone would soon after say goodbye to the music business to run a gay resort in New Jersey.

The *Bedtime Stories* Era

Bedtime Stories
Maverick: 9 45767-2
Released: October 1994
Tracklist

'Survival'	3:31
'Secret'	5:05
'I'd Rather Be Your Lover'	4:39
'Don't Stop'	4:38
'Inside of Me'	4:11
'Human Nature'	4:53
'Forbidden Love'	4:08
'Love Tried to Welcome Me'	5:21
'Sanctuary'	5:02
'Bedtime Story'	4:53
'Take a Bow'	5:21

'I'll Remember'

Maverick: 0-41355 **Single release:** March 1994 **Soundtrack:** *With Honors*
Writers: Madonna, Richard Page, Patrick Leonard
Producers: Madonna, Patrick Leonard

While many pundits remember Madonna's 1994 *Bedtime Stories* as her penance for the anti-*Sex/Erotica/Body of Evidence* backlash, the rebranding/reinvention began with this sturdy, slow burning electronic ballad with little in common to anything on *Erotica*. That's thanks, in no part, to Madonna reuniting with Leonard, while the song's original writer, Page, is best known as the lead singer for '80s big hair merchants Mr Mister. Not just crafted as a clever make-good for the public, 'I'll Remember' was

Madonna's gift to her pal Alek Keshishian as the theme song for his film *With Honors*. While the movie barely covered its budget, 'I'll Remember' returned Madonna to the US Top 10 after two misses ('Bad Girl' and 'Rain'), hit #7 in both the UK and Australia and garnered both a Grammy and Golden Globe nomination.

VID BIT!

Director: Alek Keshishian

With Honors director and Madonna BFF Keshishian delivered a slick, stylish, early Hollywood/Jazz Age clip with Madonna resembling screen siren Louise Brooks. Most viewers noted a stark similarity to the 'Rain' video, albeit with a drag of androgyny.

REMIX FIX!

After four years' absence, William Orbit got the call again for 'I'll Remember' and, if anything, provided a taster for his work to come four years later on *Ray of Light*.

'Secret'

Maverick: 9 41772-2 **Single release:** September 1994 **Album:** *Bedtime Stories*
Writers/Producers: Madonna, Dallas Austin

The next secret weapon in Madonna's bid to win back the masses and remind them she was more than just a *Sex* worker was 'Secret', the first single from her *Bedtime Stories* album. Two years after *Sex* almost killed off her *Erotica* album, Madonna's taste in music had changed. Dating basketball hero Dennis Rodman and rapper Tupac Shakur had rekindled her love of R&B music. Originally worked on as 'Something Coming Over Me' with Shep Pettibone (see Appendix I) the song was scrapped before starting over with Austin, who had found success with Boyz II Men and TLC. Madonna was also a big fan of Austin's acclaimed neo-soul work on singer/model Joi's album *The Pendulum Vibe*. Delivering a #3 US and #5 UK hit, the mellow hip-hop swagger of 'Secret' was pivotal in helping the world refocus on Madonna's music again and not her *Sex* life.

VID BIT!

Director: Melodie McDaniel

After photographing Madonna with Rodman for a *Vibe* magazine cover too hot for newsstands, McDaniel was tapped for the 'Secret' video in NYC's Harlem. A Dan-O-Rama video for the Junior Vasquez remix was also supplied.

REMIX FIX!

With Shep Pettibone literally banished by this stage, it was up to his replacement of sorts, Junior Vasquez, to bring *Secret* to the clubs. That he—hmmm mmm—did in spades!

'Let Down Your Guard'

Single release: September 1994 (B-side to 'Secret')
Writers/Producers: Madonna, Dallas Austin

The bonus track/B-side to the *Secret* CD single, 'Let Down Your Guard' creaks along like a test drive in R&B electronica which either didn't get finished properly, or was partially discarded as a leftover from girl group TLC who Austin was musically involved with (as well as eventually fathering three children with the band's Chilli). 'That's all!' a voice sounding like a heavily filtered Madonna sputters at the end. Phew.

'Survival'

Release: October 1994 **Album:** *Bedtime Stories*
Writers: Madonna, Dallas Austin
Producers: Madonna, Dallas Austin, Nellee Hooper

Battered by the press and the unrelenting personal attacks, not to mention *Erotica* being unfairly lumped in with her *Sex* book, it was a bruised Madonna who returned on her sixth album, *Bedtime Stories*. Backed with a smooth R&B groove, 'Survival' is the kinder cousin to the harsher 'Human Nature' bite back later to come on *Bedtime Stories*. 'Survival' also ushered in British producer Nellee Hooper who through his work with Sinéad O'Connor, Soul II Soul, Björk, and Massive Attack was the hottest name in the music biz. Released in late October 1994, a month after the 'Secret' single, *Bedtime Stories* hit #3 in the US, #2 in the UK and became her fifth #1 album in Australia.

'I'd Rather Be Your Lover'

Release: October 1994 **Album:** *Bedtime Stories*
Writers: Madonna, Dave Hall, Isley Brothers, Christopher Jasper
Producers: Madonna, Dave Hall

Is 'I'd Rather Be Your Lover' about Madonna's flings with Dennis Rodman, or Tupac Shakur? Featuring a sample of 'It's Your Thing' by Lou Donaldson and The Isley Brothers, Shakur's original rap was replaced by a smoking hot spoken word piece from Maverick signing Meshell Ndegeocello. Shakur's bragging 'I'd Rather Be Your Lover' rap ('what you need is a thug in your life'), nixed by his management team, emerged online decades later. The legendary rapper was killed in suspicious, unresolved circumstances in 1996. A letter he wrote while in prison to Madonna in 1995, explaining his reasons for breaking up with her, sold for over $100,000 in 2017.

'Don't Stop'

Release: October 1994 **Album:** *Bedtime Stories*
Writers: Madonna, Dallas Austin, Colin Wolfe
Producers: Madonna, Dallas Austin

Is this the greatest Madonna album track of all time never to be a single? You make that call, but 'Don't Stop' certainly did seem the obvious choice for a single from *Bedtime Stories*. While the lyrics might be a touch puerile (case in question: 'sing la-de-da-de') 'Don't Stop' is Madonna casually knocking out a premium pop song as if it's the easiest thing in the word, before just leaving it sitting there in the middle of her album waiting to be rediscovered.

'Inside of Me'

Release: October 1994 **Album:** *Bedtime Stories*
Writers: Madonna, Dave Hall, Nellee Hooper
Producers: Madonna, Nellee Hooper

Most of the *Bedtime Stories* album has sadly never been sung live. Why? Although Madonna planned to go out on the road with the album in 1995, in the meantime she snatched herself the 'role of a lifetime' as Eva Peron in the movie version of *Evita*. That meant classic cuts like the introspective 'Inside of Me' have never had their moment live on stage. Another demonstration of Madonna moving with the times, and not afraid to sample others, 'Inside of Me' included segments from three songs—'Back & Forth' by Aaliyah, 'Outstanding' by The Gap Band and 'The Trials of Life' by Gutter Snypes.

'Human Nature'

Maverick: 0-41880 **Single release:** June 1995 **Album:** *Bedtime Stories*
Writers: Madonna, Dave Hall, Shawn McKenzie, Kevin McKenzie, Michael Deering
Producers: Madonna, Dave Hall

'Express yourself, don't repress yourself!' The somewhat 'difficult' fourth single from *Bedtime Stories,* 'Human Nature' was Madonna's middle finger to those who hoped she would disappear after the *Sex* storm hit. 'Human Nature' is bitter, angry ('I didn't know I couldn't talk about sex!') and unforgiving. While it just scrapped into the UK Top 10 at #8, 'Human Nature' could not get past #46 on the US charts. Containing a sample of the bassline from 1994's rap hit 'What You Need' by hip-hop outfit Main Source, Madonna has performed 'Human Nature' on four tours including 2019–2020's *Madame X*. She also memorably performed it at the Coachella Festival in 2015 before kissing a somewhat surprised Drake onstage.

Vɪᴅ Bɪᴛ!

Director: Jean-Baptiste Mondino

Mondino was back for his third Madonna video. Going modest rather than complex, he created something unique and acerbic, even if it was simply Madonna, her dancers and her dog Chiquita in fetish gear delivering an 'absolutely no regrets!' statement. It ends with Madonna shadow boxing—and laughing.

Rᴇᴍɪx Fɪx!

Bad blood between Madonna and Junior Vasquez meant he was off the remix list. Madonna dialed up Danny Tenaglia and Satoshi Tomei for the bitchin' club mixes, while English DJ Howie Tee, offered up a set of gritty R&B mixes with samples from rapper Nine's 'Whutcha Want?' hit.

'Forbidden Love'

Release: October 1994 **Album:** *Bedtime Stories*
Writers: Madonna, Babyface
Producers: Madonna, Babyface, Nellee Hooper

Not to be confused with the song of the same title on 2005's *Confessions on a Dance Floor* album, this 'Forbidden Love' is very much Babyface-by-the-books. Clearly Madonna felt that too and brought in Hooper to add a European gloss. Including a sample of 'Down Here on the Ground' by Grant Green, 'Forbidden Love' is another track that has never had an airing outside of the studio. In April 2020, Madonna fans instigated a #JusticeForBedtimeStories campaign returning the *Bedtime Stories* album to #1 on the US iTunes Chart, albeit briefly, twenty-six years after it initially peaked at #3 on the US album charts. In response Madonna posted: 'Thank you to all my fans who got it there!! #stay home musical companion!'

'Love Tried to Welcome Me'

Release: October 1994 **Album:** *Bedtime Stories*
Writers/Producers: Madonna, Dave Hall

A swirling symphony of strings announces this welcoming R&B ballad where Madonna references Carson McCullers' *The Heart is a Lonely Hunter* and the poetry of seventeenth-century priest George Herbert. 'Most of the songs are about a kind of a spiritual struggle, or coming to terms with a spiritual struggle,' Madonna explained about *Bedtime Stories*, 'and coming to realizations about life really and there's a romantic theme too.' The real inspiration behind 'Love Tried to Welcome Me', Madonna later revealed, was actually a stripper she met at a topless bar. 'I felt sorry for her and invented her inner dialogue,' she conceded.

'Sanctuary'

Release: October 1994 **Album:** *Bedtime Stories*
Writers: Madonna, Dallas Austin, Anne Preven, Scott Cutler, Herbie Hancock
Producers: Madonna, Dallas Austin

'Sanctuary' quotes nineteenth-century poet Walt Whitman's 'Vocalism', weaves in the book of Genesis, and segues into *Bedtime Story*. Now there is a trifecta! If that was not enough, it additionally includes a sample from Hancock's 1973 electro-funk remake of his 1962 'Watermelon Man' jazz standard. 'It's about connecting to someone, to finding your soulmate, not necessarily getting married,' Madonna specified. 'Sanctuary' co-writers Preven and Cutler were members of LA rock band Ednaswap whose 1993 song 'Torn' become a global smash for Australian TV actress Natalie Imbruglia in 1997.

'Bedtime Story'

Maverick: 9 41895-2 **Single release:** February 1995 **Album:** *Bedtime Stories*
Writers: Björk, Marius De Vries, Nellee Hooper
Producers: Madonna, Nellee Hooper

While much of *Bedtime Stories* was an avid valentine to R&B, Madonna also wisely invested in some hipster electronica. Written as a 'gift' to producer pal Hooper by inimitable Icelandic artist Björk, 'Bedtime Story' signposted Madonna's future musical direction. 'Bedtime Story' was a Top 5 UK hit, where it was issued as two CD singles, the first featuring an eighteen-page booklet of drawings by Mark Bannerman as if reciting a 'bedtime story'. In the US 'Bedtime Story' was a major chart disappointment when released as the album's third single, missing the Top 40.

VID BIT!

Director: Mark Romanek

At a reported cost of $5 million, the 'Bedtime Story' video is a mind-bending eulogy to surrealism, female painters and astral travel. Fittingly it is now part of New York's Museum of Modern Art permanent collection.

REMIX FIX!

Before he got his marching orders, Junior Vasquez dominated on the remix front with his single mix chosen for the UK release, which Madonna performed at the 1995 Brit Awards with two backing dancers, in place of Björk who refused to duet with her. In March 2021, Rhino released a digital album of fourteen 'Bedtime Story' mixes.

'Take a Bow'

Maverick: 0-41887 **Single release:** December 1994 **Album:** *Bedtime Stories*
Writers/Producers: Madonna, Babyface

Madonna's biggest US hit from *Bedtime Stories* also became her longest #1 there ever, staying at the top for seven weeks. That must have taken some of the sting out of 'Take a Bow' only just managing a peak of #16 in the UK. The favourable US reaction was boosted by a live performance, sung with co-writer Babyface, on the *American Music Awards* in early 1995. Madonna also allowed it to be used that year during an episode of the *Friends* sitcom. Madonna cited '70s soft rock act Carpenters as her inspiration for 'Take a Bow', even namechecking their recording of Leon Russell's pensive 'This Masquerade'. 'Take a Bow' was a sad live omission until the Taiwanese leg of Madonna's Rebel Heart Tour in 2016 when it finally got an airing, then after sung in an acoustic version during her *Tears of a Clown* one-off show in Melbourne that same year. In 2017 *Billboard* magazine ranked 'Take a Bow' as Madonna's fourth biggest US chart hit of all time after 'Like a Virgin', 'Vogue', and 'Crazy for You'.

Vid Bit!

Director: Michael Haussman

Shot in Ronda, Spain and like a dress rehearsal (or audition tape?) for the forthcoming *Evita* movie, Madonna had never looked more like a movie star. Set in the world of bullfighting with Spanish actor/torero Emilio Muñoz playing her love interest, 'Take a Bow' won Madonna an MTV award for Best Female Video that year. Madonna sent *Evita* director Alan Parker a copy of the video, helping secure her the role of Eva Peron.

Remix Fix!

With Shep Pettibone and Junior Vasquez both off the guest list, Steve 'Silk' Hurley and InDaSoul were corralled to make 'Take a Bow' less poppy and add some urban grit. A digital pack of eight previously released mixes was issued in December 2021.

10

The *Something to Remember* Era

Something to Remember
Maverick: 9 46100-2
Released: November 1995
Tracklist

'I Want You'	6:11
'I'll Remember'	4:23
'Take a Bow'	5:21
'You'll See'	4:36
'Crazy for You'	4:11
'This Used to be My Playground'	5:10
'Live to Tell'	5:49
'Love Don't Live Here Anymore'	4:54
'Something To Remember'	5:06
'Forbidden Love'	4:09
'One More Chance'	4:28
'Rain'	5:29
'Oh Father'	4:59
'I Want You (Orchestral)'	6:04

'You'll See'

Maverick: 9 43649-2 **Single release:** October 1995 **Compilation:** *Something to Remember*
Writers/Producers: Madonna/David Foster

With that career-defining *Evita* movie title role a definite go, just ahead of Christmas Maverick released a compilation of Madonna ballads, *Something to Remember*, with three new songs. The melodramatic first single, 'You'll See', came from sessions with David Foster, who *Rolling Stone* christened 'the master of bombastic pop kitsch'. 'You'll See' proved the perfect musical segue, if not *entrée* to *Evita*. Hitting #5 in the UK, and #6 US, the song has since become a self-empowerment standard thanks to covers by Susan Boyle and Shirley Bassey.

VID BIT!

Director: Michael Haussman

'Take a Bow'—Act II! Haussman continues the sad, sorry love affair between Madonna and her grumpy-looking torero. Instead of the grand vistas of Spain though 'You'll See' was filmed on gloomy London stage sets. The more interesting Spanish version, 'Verás', added footage of Madonna recording her vocals (with lyrics by Paz Martinez).

REMIX FIX!

'Verás', the Spanish language version of 'You'll See' (also available in bilingual Spanglish), found a home on the B-side of 1996's 'One More Chance' single.

'I Want You (with Massive Attack)'

Release: November 1995 **Compilation:** *Something to Remember*
Writers: Leon Ware, Arthur 'T-Boy' Ross
Producer: Nellee Hooper

You want this—so good, Madonna included not one, but two, versions of 'I Want You' on her ballads collection. Ostensibly recorded for the *Inner City Blues: The Music of Marvin Gaye* tribute album, 'I Want You'—co-written by Diana Ross's brother, Arthur—was initially intended as *Something to Remember*'s lead single, with a video duly filmed, but nixed due to contractual issues. This masterful slice of spine-tingling pop music artistry provided the perfect sly conduit between 1994's *Bedtime Stories* and 1998's *Ray of Light*. In 2021, 'I Want You' found new appreciation as the soundtrack for a Gucci ad campaign featuring Italian Eurovision winners Måneskin.

VID BIT!

Director: Earle Sebastian

Based on the Dorothy Parker short story *A Telephone Call*, in this moody B&W clip a sultry Madonna had never had more critically revered musical companions than Massive Attack (who remain off-screen).

REMIX FIX!

Official dance versions of 'I Want You' by Junior Vasquez turned out to be bootlegs. Boo.

'One More Chance'

Maverick: 9362-43677-2 **Single release:** March 1996 **Compilation:** *Something to Remember*

Writers/Producers: Madonna, David Foster

The second of Madonna and Foster's *Something to Remember* contributions displayed her impressive new vocal chops in an earnest and endearing acoustic ballad tugging at the heartstrings. Released as a single in the UK (whose video was another cut-and-paste montage) 'One More Chance' peaked just outside the Top 10 at #11. In 2000, Mexican electropop act Sentidos Opuestos covered 'One More Chance' as 'Hoy Que No Estás'.

11

The *Evita* Era

Evita (The Complete Motion Picture Music Soundtrack)
Warner Bros. Records 9 46346-2
Released: November 1996
Tracklist
Act One/Disc One

'A Cinema in Buenos Aires, 26 July 1952'	1:20
'Requiem for Evita'	4:16
'Oh What a Circus'*	5:45
'On this Night of a Thousand Stars'	2:24
'Eva and Magaldi/Eva Beware of the City'*	5:21
'Buenos Aires'*	4:09
'Another Suitcase in Another Hall'*	3:33
'Goodnight and Thank You'*	4:18
'The Lady's Got Potential'	4:25
'Charity Concert/The Art of the Possible'*	2:33
'I'd Be Surprisingly Good for You'*	4:19
'Hello and Goodbye'*	1:47
'Peron's Latest Flame'*	5:17
'A New Argentina'*	8:10

Act Two/Disc Two

'On the Balcony of the Casa Rosada 1'	1:29
'Don't Cry for Me Argentina*'	5:31
'On The Balcony of the Casa Rosada 2'*	2:00
'High Flying Adored'*	3:32
'Rainbow High'*	2:27
'Rainbow Tour'*	4:51
'The Actress Hasn't Learned the Lines (You'd Like to Hear)'*	2:32
'And the Money Kept Rolling In (And Out)'	3:53

'Partido Feminista'*	1:40
'She is a Diamond'	1:40
'Santa Evita'	2:31
'Waltz for Eva and Che'*	4:13
'Your Little Body's Slowly Breaking Down'*	1:25
'You Must Love Me'*	2:51
'Eva's Final Broadcast'*	3:05
'Latin Chant'	2:11
'Lament'*	5:17

Tracks featuring some portion of Madonna vocals.

Also released in October 1997 as a single disc version *Evita (Music from the Motion Picture)* on Warner Bros. Records 9362-46432-2

'You Must Love Me'

Warner Bros. Records: 9 17495-2 **Single release:** October 1996 **Soundtrack:** *Evita*
Writers: Andrew Lloyd Webber, Tim Rice
Producers: Madonna, Nigel Wright, Alan Parker, Andrew Lloyd Webber, David Caddick

Evita was the biggest movie moment of Madonna's career, either before or since. Eva Peron was the role Madonna was born to play and play it so well did she it earned her a Golden Globe for Best Actress. While an Oscar, or Oscar nomination, sadly eluded Madonna, her emotive performance of the one new song written for the movie, 'You Must Love Me', won the Oscar for Best Original Song. Released as the first single from *Evita*, 'You Must Love Me' went to #10 in the UK and #18 in the US. After nervously performing it at the Academy Awards in 1997 as a new first-time mother, Madonna only ever sang it on 2008's Sticky & Sweet Tour as an acoustic gypsy-style ballad. *Evita* director/soundtrack co-producer Parker died in 2020 after a lengthy illness. Madonna paid him tribute saying he 'pushed me to my limits and made an incredible film! Thank you!'

VID BIT!
Director: Alan Parker

Pregnant Madonna sings earnestly beside a piano and a string quartet intercut with scenes from *Evita*. It looks like movie magic and it is! *Evita* was a box office blockbuster, as was the soundtrack—both versions.

REMIX FIX!
The 'You Must Love Me' single included a bonus Orchestral Version segueing seamlessly into 'I'd Be Surprisingly Good for You'. Well-tuned eardrums to this 'Evita Suite' will spot a brief guitar refrain of 'Don't Cry for Me Argentina'.

'Rainbow High'

Single release: October 1996 (B-side to 'You Must Love Me') **Soundtrack:** *Evita*
Writers: Andrew Lloyd Webber, Tim Rice
Producers: Nigel Wright, Alan Parker, Andrew Lloyd Webber, David Caddick

Just a little touch of star quality! The B-side for 'You Must Love Me' is the only other Madonna solo number from *Evita*, besides the three hits and one club smash, to receive a single release. According to the *Guinness Book of World Records*, as Eva Peron in *Evita* Madonna holds the record for 'Most Costume Changes in a Film' (eighty-five to be precise) and a large number of those feature in the 'Rainbow High' sequence.

'Don't Cry For Me Argentina'

Warner Bros. Records: 9 43809-2 **Single release:** December 1996 **Soundtrack:** *Evita*
Writers: Andrew Lloyd Webber, Tim Rice
Producers: Nigel Wright, Alan Parker, Andrew Lloyd Webber, David Caddick

After working with a vocal coach for six months to develop her upper register, Madonna was ready to embody Eva Peron. On the first day of recording in London though, after belting out 'Don't Cry for Me Argentina' in front of an orchestra, Madonna left in tears. She subsequently recorded her vocals in a separate studio, but those voice lessons sure paid off. Originally a worldwide #1 (with the exception of the US) in 1976 for Julie Covington, 'Don't Cry for Me Argentina' became a musical theatre standard. Could Madonna do it justice? Could she ever! Madonna's version was a Top 10 hit in the US and #3 in the UK. In 2020, Madonna performed 'DCFMA' *a cappella* for Andrew Lloyd Webber, in the audience watching her *Madame X* show at the London Palladium (which he also owns) wryly informing the crowd, 'he was a tough taskmaster but he taught me well.' Near its twenty-fifth anniversary in late 2021, the single was finally certified gold for UK sales of 400,000.

VID BIT!
Director: Alan Parker

Why make a video when you have the perfect sequence from *Evita* to use?

REMIX FIX!

Madonna rerecorded her vocals for the Latin-loving club/Spanglish Miami Mix of 'Don't Cry for Me Argentina' conceived by Pablo Flores and Javier Garza.

'Another Suitcase in Another Hall'

Warner Bros. Records: 9362 43847-2 **Single release:** March 1997 **Soundtrack:** *Evita*
Writers: Andrew Lloyd Webber, Tim Rice
Producers: Nigel Wright, Alan Parker, Andrew Lloyd Webber, David Caddick

Madonna knew a good song when she heard one, insisting the movie script of *Evita* be changed so she could warble 'Another Suitcase in Another Hall'. Originally a UK #18 hit for Barbara Dickson in 1977, as the third official *Evita* single, 'Another Suitcase in Another Hall' did better second time round—hitting #7 in the UK charts, but went unreleased in the US.

Vid Bit!

Director: Alan Parker

Again, why spend good money on a video when you already have the *Evita* epic?

Remix Fix!

A rumour about 'Another Suitcase in Another Hall' remixes was just another rumour.

'Buenos Aires'

Warner Bros. Records: PRO-A-8984-A **Promo release:** October 1997 **Soundtrack:** *Evita*
Writers: Andrew Lloyd Webber, Tim Rice
Producers: Nigel Wright, Alan Parker, Andrew Lloyd Webber, David Caddick

What's new? Another Madonna solo song from *Evita* that almost became a single! Remixers Javier Garza and Pablo Flores cut loose on this fine soundtrack cut too, turning it into a peak hour Latin house jam. Warner Bros sent out promos for the little touch of star quality Te Amo mixes in 1997, tying in with *Evita*'s home video release. Despite no official release, 'Buenos Aires' hit #3 on the US Dance Club Song chart.

12

The Ray of Light Era

Ray of Light
Maverick: 9 46847-2
Released: February 1998
Tracklist

'Drowned World/Substitute for Love'	5:09
'Swim'	5:00
'Ray of Light'	5:21
'Candy Perfume Girl'	4:34
'Skin'	6:22
'Nothing Really Matters'	4:27
'Sky Fits Heaven'	4:48
'Shanti/Ashtangi'	4:29
'Frozen'	6:12
'The Power of Good-Bye'	4:10
'To Have and Not to Hold'	5:23
'Little Star'	5:18
'Mer Girl'	5:32
Japanese Bonus Track	
'Has to Be'	5:15

'Frozen'

Maverick: 9 43993-2 **Single release:** February 1998 **Album:** *Ray of Light*
Writers: Madonna, Patrick Leonard,
Producers: Madonna, Patrick Leonard, William Orbit
   'For "Frozen" I was obsessed with the movie *The Sheltering Sky*,' Madonna
recalled, 'so I told Pat I wanted something with a tribal feel, something really

lush and romantic.' With the rudimentary melody written by Madonna and Leonard (i.e. 'Pat'), 'Frozen' was transformed by Orbit into something both slightly sinister and supremely seductive. While Orbit's sonics reverberated as otherworldly, ethereal and esoteric, the unequivocal fact is 'Frozen' is a majestic pop song. The startlingly emotive strings, arranged by Craig Armstrong, only added to its glacial charms. While 'Frozen' battled Celine Dion's titanic 'My Heart Will Go On' for top spot on the charts upon release (#2 US and #1 UK), it provided the perfect launch pad for Madonna's earnest, empathetic earth mother *Ray of Light* masterpiece. During 2019–2020's Madame X Tour, 'Frozen' became a spine-tingling highlight with now grown-up daughter Lourdes executing an interpretative dance with the initials 'M O M' on her hands.

VID BIT!

Director: Chris Cunningham

Shot in the Mojave Desert, employing plenty of CGI trickery, the 'Frozen' video went on to win an MTV Music Video Award for Best Special Effects.

REMIX FIX!

Stereo MC's took a languid, underground approach, but Victor Calderone's killer Club Mix added drama, while staying true to our reborn mother goddess/Kabbalah raver. In March 2021, Rhino released a digital album of ten 'Frozen' mixes, and later that same year, courtesy of TikTok, a 'sickhop' Madonna x Sickick remix was officially released. Madonna reportedly worked on a new version of 'Frozen' with Swae Lee in early 2022.

'Shanti/Ashtangi'

Single release: February 1998 (B-side to 'Frozen') **Album:** *Ray of Light*
Writers/Producers: Madonna, William Orbit

If 'Frozen' signalled a new Madonna, if not a new age Madonna, what about its flipped out, dippy hippy B-side 'Shanti/Ashtangi'? 'This song was inspired by the Sanskrit prayers we chant before we do yoga,' Madonna explained at the time of the album's release. 'The saying of Sanskrit is as important as the meaning of it. Every time I say it, it makes me feel good and I felt inspired by that and wanted to put it on my record.' To feel competent, Madonna took a crash course in Sanskrit and using her 'artistic license' wove in two Vedic prayers from the thirteenth century 'and I threw in a bunch of stuff too. I wanted to take the idea of it and put it into the 21st century and use modern sound.' Namaste.

'Drowned World/Substitute for Love'

Maverick: 5439-17156-9 **Single release:** August 1998 **Album:** *Ray of Light*
Writers: Madonna, William Orbit, Rod McKuen, Anita Kerr, David Collins
Producers: Madonna, William Orbit

'And now I find I've changed my mind/This is my religion!' The opening song on *Ray of Light* presaged not just a change in musical direction for Madonna, but a change in artistic attitude and world view. The ambient pop 'Drowned World/Substitute for Love', issued as a single outside of the US, was based on a poem her friend, London interior designer Collins, wrote for her. McKuen and Kerr were given songwriting credits due to a sample of 'Why I Follow the Tigers' from the San Sebastian Strings, featuring the voice of actor Bobby Pearson ('You see') who narrated albums for the pair. The term 'drowned world' derived from the 1962 science-fiction novel of the same name from author J. G. Ballard about a time when global warming has made the earth uninhabitable. Madonna called 'Drowned World/Substitute for Love' the most important song on her album, which is why in 2001 she coined her Drowned World Tour. 'The song addresses the idea of fame,' Madonna explained. In the UK, the single entered and peaked at #10, while hitting #1 in Spain. Madonna graciously granted Collins a co-writing credit on the track, dedicating it to his memory in London on 2015's Rebel Heart Tour, two years after he died of complications from AIDs.

VID BIT!
Director: Walter Stern

Filmed in London in June 1998, Stern's rumination on the fame monster encapsulated Madonna being chased by paparazzi in street scenes evocative of Princess Diana who had died less than a year earlier though—hurrah!—it ends with Madonna finding comfort in her true love's arms, her daughter (played by a child actor).

REMIX FIX!
The 'Drowned World/Substitute for Love' mixes might not have been to everyone's clubbing taste, but included on the B-side were much more dance floor friendly remixes of 'Sky Fits Heaven' from Victor Calderone and Sasha.

'Swim'

Release: February 1998 **Album:** *Ray of Light*
Writers/Producers: Madonna, William Orbit

'The birth of my daughter was a kind of rebirth for me,' Madonna said in 1998, 'and I looked at life in a completely new way. That made me appreciate life in a way I don't think I ever had before.' That was more than evident on *Ray of Light*'s second track, 'Swim', where Madonna (later to use her Hebrew name of Esther briefly) sang about being baptized by the healing power of water to 'wash away all our sins'. 'Swim' also features one of Madonna's most touchingly vulnerable vocals. That day, 15 July 1997, it transpires, she had just been told her friend, designer Gianni Versace, was dead. 'We were recording "Swim" on the day Versace was murdered,' Orbit revealed in 2002 to *Q Magazine*, 'which is probably why it has such an emotional impact.'

'Ray of Light'

Maverick: 936244536 2 **Single release:** May 1998 **Album:** *Ray of Light*
Writers: Madonna, William Orbit, Clive Maldoon, Dave Curtiss, Christine Leach
Producers: Madonna, William Orbit

The second single from the album of the same name, 'Ray of Light' is based on parts of 1971's 'Sepheryn' from English folk music duo Curtiss Maldoon, rerecorded in 1996 by Maldoon's niece, Christine Leach, with Orbit, then sent to Madonna as a demo. Madonna loved it, rewrote some lyrics and the newly retitled 'Ray of Light' ran for over ten minutes, eventually trimmed to just over half that. A trailblazing piece of music managing to be pop song, rock song, ambient electronica, and, more than all of those parts combined, 'Ray of Light' appealed to a whole new generation. 'I feel it has a really hopeful message to it,' Madonna gushed. As a single, 'Ray of Light' peaked at #2 in the UK and #5 in the US, becoming the year's biggest dance song stateside. In 2020, U2's Bono cited 'Ray of Light' as one of the sixty songs that changed his life.

Vid Bit!

Director: Jonas Åkerlund

A Grammy winner for Best Short Form Music Video, Åkerlund's 'Ray of Light' video also won five MTV Music Video Awards. The *Ray of Light* video proved to be as timely as it was timeless, just like the song itself.

Remix Fix!

Orbit's swinging '60s Ultra Violet Mix, importantly, would be a template for 1999's 'Beautiful Stranger' hit. Decisively, 'Ray of Light' won the Grammy in 1999 for Best Dance Recording.

'Candy Perfume Girl'

Release: February 1998 **Album:** *Ray of Light*
Writers: Madonna, William Orbit, Susannah Melvoin
Producers: Madonna, William Orbit

Madonna tried out a number of songwriters for the *Ray of Light* project including Babyface before, as he put it diplomatically, she 'changed her idea about the album's direction'. One of the album's quirkiest and queerest tracks is 'Candy Perfume Boy', co-written with former Prince fiancée/band member Melvoin. In an interview with *Rolling Stone*, Melvoin revealed she wrote the psychedelia-inspired 'Candy Perfume Girl' with Orbit while mourning the death of her brother, Jonathan, in 1996 from a heroin overdose 'and the allure of drug addiction'. She also claimed to have written most of the lyrics for 'Swim' but was not given credit.

'Skin'

Release: February 1998 **Album:** *Ray of Light*
Writers: Madonna, Patrick Leonard
Producers: Madonna, William Orbit, Marius de Vries

The true charm of the *Ray of Light* album is not cherry-picking the singles, or examining each track individually, but how as a cohesive body of work it takes the listener on a journey through Madonna's heart, soul and spirit. Originally called 'Flirtation Dance' (a more Eastern leaning demo is available online), 'Skin' is Madonna reconnecting to her life-long exploration of the sensual world. 'I feel like I am moving more and more into the spiritual area in terms of exploring, which is not to say that I'm not interested in sex,' she smirked.

REMIX FIX!
Club 69 gave 'Skin' a suitably sleazy gay leather bar polish for DJ remixes, while The Collaboration Remix, saw Club 69 teaming up with Victor Calderone.

'Nothing Really Matters'

Maverick: 9 44613-2 **Single release:** March 1999 **Album:** *Ray of Light*
Writers: Madonna, Patrick Leonard
Producers: Madonna, William Orbit, Marius de Vries

Inspired by the birth of her daughter Lourdes/Lola, the fifth and final Kabbalah-esque single from *Ray of Light*, released in March 1999, was also its biggest gay club hit. While it stiffed on the US chart at #93 due to lack of airplay and CD single release delays, 'Nothing Really Matters' went to a more deserving #7 in the UK. One of its most laudable features is the dynamic backing vocals of Niki Haris and Donna De Lory.

VID BIT!
Director: Johan Renck

Wrapped in a Jean-Paul Gaultier red kimono as if auditioning for the *Memoirs Of A Geisha* movie (eventually made in 2005 with an Asian cast), drag queens adored the outlandish 'Nothing Really Matters' video (see season eight of *RuPaul's Drag Race*). A Dan-O-Rama remix video, set to Club 69's futuristic dance beat, helped solidify that. Renck won an Emmy in 2019 for directing the *Chernobyl* mini-series.

REMIX FIX!
Peter Rauhofer's Club 69 batch overshadowed all as queer-friendly club smashes.

'Sky Fits Heaven'

Single release: August 1998 (B-side to 'Drowned World/Substitute for Love')
Album: *Ray of Light*
Writers: Madonna, Patrick Leonard
Producers: Madonna, William Orbit, Patrick Leonard

Turned down by Tricky, Goldie, The Prodigy, and Massive Attack, Madonna eventually found her perfect collaborator in Orbit. 'I know how to write a good pop song with hooks,' she pointed out, so she combined those elements with techno music, but 'wanted to make it intimate and emotional.' 'Sky Fits Heaven' is yet another bold experiment where Madonna's American influences clash head on with Orbit's European sensibilities creating something that folds and weaves together like a magic carpet. Released as the B-side to the 'Drowned World/Substitute for Love' single, 'Sky Fits Heaven' snuck into the US dance charts via the Sasha and Victor Calderone mixes from import copy play alone. The opening lyrics of 'Sky Fits Heaven' were from a spoken word piece, 'What Fits', poet Max Blagg recited in a 1993 Gap jeans TV ad. Madonna contacted Blagg early on in the *Ray of Light* project to work out a financial arrangement to re-voice his words.

'The Power of Good-bye'

Maverick: 5439-17121-9 **Single release:** September 1998 **Album:** *Ray of Light*
Writers: Madonna, Rick Nowels
Producers: Madonna, William Orbit, Patrick Leonard

After having just snared 1997's Album of the Year Grammy for Celine Dion's *Falling Into You*, Nowels introduced himself to Madonna in NYC out shopping at luxury department store Barneys. Soon after they wrote three songs for *Ray of Light* including the album's elegant and ethereal third US single, 'The Power of Good-bye'. It is hard not to imagine with new mother Madonna ending the relationship with her child's father, personal trainer Carlos Leon, this did not influence 'The Power of Good-Bye''s heartfelt subject matter. This powerful ballad, which *Billboard* called 'underrated', peaked at #11 in the US, but reached #6 in the UK.

Vid Bit!
Director: Matthew Rolston

An homage to 1946 movie *Humoresque* starring screen vamp Joan Crawford, Madonna, like Crawford's character, vanishes into the ocean. Co-starring future *ER* hunk Goran Višnjić as Madonna's chess-playing love interest, 'The Power of Good-bye' video is moodily epic and visually stunning.

Remix Fix!
More experimental than empowering, Luke Slater twisted 'The Power of Good-bye' into a hectic techno nightmare, Fabien Waltmann conjured a drum 'n' bass makeover and Dallas Austin crafted a breakbeat-heavy reproduction.

'To Have and Not to Hold'

Release: February 1998 **Album:** *Ray of Light*
Writers: Madonna, Rick Nowels
Producers: Madonna, Patrick Leonard, William Orbit

The second of three Nowels co-writes on *Ray of Light* exposes Madonna as a 'moth to a flame' with a hypnotic tribal-meets-bossa nova beat. The new yoga devotee even tossed in a chant of '*abahu purusakaram*' (rough translation: 'the one who attains true self through strength'), used as the Ashtanga opening mantra in Shanti Yoga and Ayurveda. Sublimely melding Orbit's moody sonic soundscape with some of Madonna's most poetic lyrics ('To look but not to see/ To kiss but never be') 'To Have and Not to Hold' is yet another highlight in an album teeming with them.

'Little Star'

Release: February 1998 **Album:** *Ray of Light*
Writers: Madonna, Rick Nowels
Producers: Madonna, Marius de Vries

When word first spread about Madonna's new album post-*Evita* and post-baby there was consternation it would an album of lullabies. If anything comes close to that description its 'Little Star', a love song for her new baby daughter. Madonna sang 'Little Star' live in a stripped-down acoustic version on Oprah during the initial promotion for the *Ray of Light* album, but has never sung it since. 'Little Star', and the bigger *Ray of Light* album, inspired another new mum, Adele, to write her hugely successful 25 album in 2015. 'That's the record Madonna wrote after having her first child,' Adele told *Rolling Stone*, 'and for me, it's her best.' *Ray of Light* would be nominated for six Grammys in 1999, winning four including Best Pop Album. A dreamy demo of 'Little Star' pre-dating Orbit, leaked in 2019.

'Mer Girl'

Release: February 1998 **Album:** *Ray of Light*
Writers/Producers: Madonna, William Orbit

Just when you thought you had heard all there was for Madonna to say, and sing, about the death of her mother, here tumbles 'Mer Girl', *Ray of Light*'s thirteenth track (Madonna thought it a lucky number) and album closer. For 'Mer Girl' Madonna decided she would 'write a song to the music as given to me … I said, "I want it just like it is, I want you to put the tape up right now and I'm gonna sing to it!"' 'Mer Girl' was performed in two halves with 'Sky Fits Heaven' on the Drowned World Tour.

'Has to Be'

Single release: May 1998 (B-side to 'Ray of Light') **Album (Japan only):** *Ray of Light*
Writers: Madonna, Patrick Leonard, William Orbit
Producers: Madonna, William Orbit

Removed from *Ray of Light* because it would be track 14 (Kabbalah refers to the thirteen rungs on the heavenly ladder), 'Has to Be' reappeared as the 'Ray of Light' single B-side and on the Japanese album. Originally a more traditional piano ballad written by Madonna and Leonard (as a demo online proves), the hurting yet hopeful trip-hop electronica of 'Has to Be' is a fan favourite Madonna has lamentably never performed. In 2021, Leonard finally sold the music publishing for his songs for a 'multi-million dollar' figure.

13

The *Next Best Thing* and Other Things Era

The Next Best Thing (Music from the Motion Picture)
Maverick: 9 47595-2
Released: February 2000
Tracklist

Métisse	'Boom Boom Ba'	3:41
Manu Chao	'Bongo Bong'	2:55
Christina Aguilera	'Don't Make Me Love You ('Til I'm Ready)'	3:39
Madonna	'American Pie'	4:33
Mandalay	'This Life'	4:18
Groove Armada	'If Everybody Looked the Same'	3:39
Moby	'Why Does My Heart Feel So Bad?'	4:23
Beth Orton	'Stars All Seem to Weep'	4:39
Madonna	'Time Stood Still'	3:48
Solar Twins	'Swayambhu'	3:07
Gabriel Yared	'Forever and Always'	6:00

'If You Forget Me'

Miramax Records: MH-62029-2 **Release:** June 1995 **Compilation:**
The Postman/Il Postino
Writer: Pablo Neruda

The Postman (Il Postino): Music from the Miramax Motion Picture featured artists reciting poems by Chilean Nobel Prize winner Pablo Neruda. Madonna tackled the thoughtful 'If You Forget Me' ('everything carries me to you'), with other poetry readers included Glenn Close, Sting, Julia Roberts, and Samuel L. Jackson. This compilation, plus its Oscar winning soundtrack by Luis Enriquez Bacalov, were put together by Miramax, at the time headed by the now infamous Harvey Weinstein.

'Guilty By Association' (Joe Henry & Madonna)

Columbia: CK 67573 **Release:** August 1996 **Compilation:** *Sweet Relief II: Gravity of the Situation*
Writer: Vic Chestnutt
Producers: Joe Henry, Patrick McCarthy

Something of a buried obscurity, 'Guilty by Association' is eminent as the first instance Madonna recorded with brother-in-law Henry (married to her sister Melanie). Their alt-country ballad duet was mustered for the charity album *Sweet Relief II: Gravity of the Situation*, interpreting the songs of Chestnutt to benefit healthcare for musicians. Ironically, Chestnutt wrote the song about the albatross of his friend R.E.M.'s Michael Stipe celebrity, who also originally appeared on it.

'Freedom'

RCA Victor: RCMJ 44769-2 **Release:** April 1997 **Compilation:** *Carnival! The Rainforest Foundation*
Writers/Producers: Madonna, Dallas Austin

A discarded track from the 1994 *Bedtime Stories* album, 'Freedom' might have been a precursor for that album's *Secret*. Opening with a similar guitar riff, Madonna sings lyrics about justice that have not dated so well ('No is just a word people say when they are afraid/And if you say no to me then I will fight you till I'm free') complete with a gospel-lite backing. Barely over three minutes long, 'Freedom' is a Prince-esque curio that surfaced on the *Carnival! The Rainforest Foundation* charity album, alongside tracks by Sting, Elton John and Annie Lennox.

'Bittersweet' (Deepak & Friends)

Rasā Music: RSCD3078 Release: September 1998 Compilation: *A Gift of Love: Music Inspired by the Love Poems of Rumi*
Writers: Adam Plack, Deepak Chopra
Producer: Adam Plack

If Madonna had piqued people's interest in further spiritual enlightenment after *Ray of Light*, this track from the *A Gift of Love: Music Inspired by the Love Poems of Rumi* album made a gentle entry point. Credited to Guru Deepak Chopra (as Deepak & Friends) 'Bittersweet''s ambient, downtempo extract is very much Kabbalah-lite, produced by Australian didgeridoo player Plack. Others who contributed to this collection of poetry from thirteenth Sufi mystic Rumi included Demi Moore, Goldie Hawn, and civil rights activist Rosa Parks.

'Be Careful (Cuidado Con Mi Corazón)' (Ricky Martin duet with Madonna)

Columbia: CK 69891 **Release:** May 1999 **Album:** *Ricky Martin*
Writers/Producers: Madonna, William Orbit

Released one week before Madonna's 'Beautiful Stranger' single, this sumptuous duet with Ricky Martin is one of the great unsung Madonna songs. After witnessing Ricky Martin perform at the 1999 Grammy Awards, Madonna recorded 'Be Careful' with Martin for his English language debut album together with Orbit. Due to record company wrangling, 'Be Careful' was never released as a single. A stunning solo demo of 'Be Careful', with Madonna singing mostly in Spanish, leaked a decade later.

'Beautiful Stranger'

Maverick: 9362 44699-2 **Single release:** May 1999 **Soundtrack:** *Austin Powers: The Spy Who Shagged Me*
Writers/Producers: Madonna, William Orbit

Yeah, baby! Taking its starting point from 'Ray of Light''s Ultra Violet Mix, 'Beautiful Stranger' perfectly slotted into the 'Britpop' wave of the late 1990s (though vaguely redolent of Love's 'She Comes in Colors' from 1966). Never confirmed nor denied, but the actual 'beautiful stranger' in the song was British writer Andy Bird who Madonna dated prior to meeting Guy Ritchie. A #2 UK hit and #17 in the US (based on radio play only as Warner chose not to release a CD single), Madonna performed 'Beautiful Stranger' on 2001's Drowned World Tour and on the final date pulled new husband Ritchie on stage. She next sang it, post-divorce, at her *Send in the Clowns* show in Miami in 2016.

VID BIT!

Director: Brett Ratner

The chemistry between Madonna and her old comedy pal Mike Myers was the perfect sales pitch for *Austin Powers: The Spy Who Shagged Me*, which grossed over $312 million. So good was the 'Beautiful Stranger' video, it won a Grammy.

REMIX FIX!

While the original 'Beautiful Stranger' was too rocky, indie, or quirky for the club crowd, Victor Calderone converted it into a stomping dance floor filler. In May 2021, Rhino issued a five-track remix EP (four by Calderone plus Orbit's radio edit) digitally.

'American Pie'

Maverick: 9362448372 **Single release:** March 2000 **Soundtrack:** *The Next Best Thing*
Writer: Don McLean
Producers: Madonna, William Orbit

Was there ever a Madonna song that more divided fans and critics alike? Madonna's first single of the noughties was a cover of rock classic 'American Pie', a #1 hit for its writer McLean in 1971. Coaxed into recording it for the soundtrack to their movie *The Next Best Thing* by co-star Rupert Everett, Madonna's version reached #1 in the UK, Australia, Germany, Italy, Norway, and many other countries. Not released as a single in the US, 'American Pie' nonetheless hit #29 on radio play alone. McLean called Madonna's cover 'a gift from a goddess', though reviewers were less impressed with Madonna's truncated treatment of an American classic ('sub-karaoke fluff' was the *NME*'s complaint). Because it sold so well, 'American Pie' was added as a bonus track to her next album *Music*.

Vid Bit!

Director: Philipp Stölzl

In what was like a giddier, queerer forerunner of 2003's revised 'American Life' video, Madonna dances in front of the American flag in a tiara mixed in with scenes of modern Americana including LGBT couples kissing. A second Dan-O-Rama version of the 'American Pie' clip, to accompany the Humpty Remix, featured additional footage, no gay or lesbian kisses and Rupert Everett attempting background vocals.

Remix Fix!

While Richard 'Humpty' Vission added pop-dance fizz, it was Victor Calderone who made this a club staple, which virtually obliterated the melody and lyrics.

'Time Stood Still'

Release: February 2000 **Soundtrack:** *The Next Best Thing*
Writers/Producers: Madonna, William Orbit

Another of the 'great disremembered Madonna B-sides', Madonna found time to toss this off as an extra track for *The Next Best Thing* soundtrack. 'Time Stood Still' does still stand as one of Madonna's loveliest ballads, later reworked by Ellie Lawson as 'Inside Out' on her 2005 album *The Philosophy Tree*. After being given a set of Orbit instrumentals to work on, Lawson wrote a lyric for one before discovering 'Time Stood Still' already existed as a song and Madonna's blessing was required.

14

The *Music*/*GHV2* Era

Music
Maverick: 9362-47865-2
Released: September 2000
Tracklist

'Music'	3:45
'Impressive Instant'	3:37
'Runaway Lover'	4:47
'I Deserve It'	4:23
'Amazing'	3:43
'Nobody's Perfect'	4:58
'Don't Tell Me'	4:40
'What It Feels Like for a Girl'	4:43
'Paradise (Not For Me)'	6:33
'Gone'	3:29

International Edition bonus track

'American Pie'	4:36

Japanese and Australian bonus track

'Cyber-Raga'	5:33

Mexican bonus tracks

'Lo Que Siente La Mujer (What It Feels Like for a Girl)'	4:44
'What It Feels Like For A Girl' (Above & Beyond Club Radio Edit)	3:45

GHV2 (Greatest Hits Volume 2)
Maverick: 9362-48000-2
Released: November 2001
Tracklist

'Deeper and Deeper' (7" Edit)	4:54
'Erotica' (Radio Edit)	4:33

'Human Nature' (Radio Version)	4:31
'Secret' (Edit)	4:30
'Don't Cry for Me Argentina' (Radio Edit)	4:50
'Bedtime Story' (Edit)	4:07
'The Power of Good-Bye'	4:11
'Beautiful Stranger' (William Orbit Radio Edit)	3:57
'Frozen' (Edit)	5:09
'Take a Bow' (Edit)	4:31
'Ray of Light' (Radio Edit)	4:35
'Don't Tell Me'	4:40
'What It Feels Like for a Girl'	4:44
'Drowned World/Substitute for Love'	5:09
'Music'	3:45

'Paradise (Not for Me)' (Mirwais/Madonna)

Naïve: NV 3151-1 **Release:** April/September 2000 **Mirwais album:** *Production*
Madonna album: *Music*
Writers/Producers: Mirwais Ahmadzaï, Madonna

Before there was 'Music' there was 'Paradise' for Madonna, or not, as the title suggests. Released six months before the *Music* album in April 2000 as an album track on *Production*, the second solo album by Mirwais, 'Paradise (Not for Me)' gave Madonna fans and fanatics alike an early warning she refused to play safe and was not intent on merely sticking with a winner in Orbit. Partly sung in French, steeped in a near electro-dirge ambiance and soon after included on her *Music* album, 'Paradise (Not for Me)' is one of the strangest Madonna songs of all time, and therein lies its charm. When Madonna performed her *Tears of a Clown* shows in 2016 in Melbourne and Miami, 'Paradise (Not for Me)' was one of the songs she gratifyingly wallowed in.

'Music'

Maverick: 9 44909-2 **Single release:** August 2000 **Album:** *Music*
Writers/Producers: Madonna, Mirwais Ahmadzaï

Two years after the most critically acclaimed album of her career Madonna delivered her eighth studio album, *Music,* preceded by its thrillingly innovative single of the same name. 'Almost without warning, I felt like I needed to explode,' Madonna recounted. 'I felt like dancing.' Madonna did so with a new music man in her life, Mirwais Ahmadzaï. After being talent-spotted by Madonna's business partner and future manager Guy Oseary, 'Music' blended his boogie woogie with

Madonna's lyrical epiphany about the healing power of music, after attending a Sting concert. Released in August 2000, a month before the album of the same name, Madonna's 'Music' single reached #1 in 25 countries and still stands as her last US #1. Nominated for a Record of the Year Grammy, 'Music' became Madonna's ninth biggest US hit, according to *Billboard*.

Vid Bit!

Director: Jonas Åkerlund

Initially Madonna requested comedian Chris Rock for *Music*, but Åkerlund suggested Sacha Baron Cohen in character as rapper Ali G. Åkerlund recalls the biggest issue for the shoot being 'fedora or cowboy hat?' Shot in LA at the Charlie Chaplin studio the team walked across the road to a strip club to film (s)extra scenes.

Remix Fix!

Madonna's longest running US dance #1 (a staggering five weeks) came complete with remixes from Groove Armada, Deep Dish, Victor Calderone, Tracy Young (her first for Madonna), Hex Hector & Mac Quayle, Richard 'Humpty' Vission, and Robbie Rivera.

'Cyber-Raga'

Single release: August 2000 (B-side to 'Music') **Album:** *Music*
Writers/Producers: Madonna, Talvin Singh

The B-side to the 'Music' single (and a bonus track on *Music* in some territories) 'Cyber-Raga' has all the hallmarks of a bungled cyber-collaboration. Considered the father of modern Asian electronica, Singh had previously remixed 'Nothing Really Matters' from Madonna's *Ray of Light* album into a lavish but cluttered eastern escapade. 'Cyber-Raga' was more of the same as Madonna devoutly recited a spiritual passage in Sanskrit requesting the leaders of the world protect the earth. Truth told, 'Cyber-Raga' is as problematic to listen to as its title suggests. Madonna resurrected it surprisingly successfully, however, for 2012's MDNA Tour.

'Impressive Instant'

Maverick: PRO-A-100771 **Promo release:** September 2001 **Album:** *Music*
Writers/Producers: Madonna, Mirwais Ahmadzaï

The initial Madonna/Mirwais alliance hit a roadblock due to an unforeseen language barrier—Mirwais barely spoke any English. His manager had to turn translator before 'Impressive Instant', M&M's first joint work, could slide into view. 'Impressive Instant' was Madonna's choice for a fourth *Music* single, sent out to clubs with remixes from Peter Rauhofer. The impressive, sexed-up big room thumper, minus some of the song's more dubious lyrics ('I like to singy singy singy/Like a bird on a wingy wingy wing'), hit #1 for two weeks on *Billboard*'s Dance Club Songs chart.

'Runaway Lover'

Release: September 2000 **Album:** *Music*
Writers/Producers: Madonna, William Orbit
'Runaway Lover' found Orbit playing catch-up next to Mirwais's hipster electropop. Not that it mattered too much to Orbit, or his accountant presumably. After his ground-breaking work on their trippy, hippychick electronica opus *Ray of Light*, Orbit subsequently lent his producer skills to artists such as Blur, P!nk, All Saints , U2, and former Spice Girl Mel C. Madonna only ever performed 'Runaway Lover' live during her November 2000, mini-club gigs in New York (wearing a tank top emblazoned with 'Britney Spears') and London (changing the top to read new son 'Rocco') streamed live on the internet.

'I Deserve It'

Release: September 2000 **Album:** *Music*
Writers/Producers: Madonna, Mirwais Ahmadzaï
Giddily in love and prepping to give birth to son Rocco in August that year, Madonna was more than entitled to compose a love song for her new soon-to-be husband Guy Ritchie. 'This guy was made for me/And I was made for him' she swooned, insisting all the pain from the past was worth it now. Ah yes, the honeymoon phase! It was deservedly performed during 2001's Drowned World Tour with Madonna accompanying herself on guitar. After the tour Ritchie directed his new wife in the movie *Swept Away*, a critical and commercial disaster. Madonna and Ritchie never worked together again, they divorced in 2008 and Madonna never sang 'I Deserve It' again.

'Amazing'

Release: September 2000 **Album:** *Music*
Writers/Producers: Madonna, William Orbit
'Amazing', which Madonna called her 'I-love-you-but-fuck-you' song, resembled a slightly harsher rehash of the previous year's 'Beautiful Stranger', a fact not lost

on *zeitgeist*-conscious Madonna. At the time, 'Amazing' fit amazingly into radio programs with its jolly Britpop sensibility and Orbit still flavour of the month. It seemed a dead cert as a single. Her record label thought so too, servicing the song to radio in advance of a video from Madonna's then upcoming Drowned World Tour. Madonna, not to be crossed, axed 'Amazing' from her set list. In retrospect 'Amazing' was two years too late and Madonna did her due diligence well.

'Nobody's Perfect'

Release: September 2000 **Album:** *Music*
Writers/Producers: Madonna, Mirwais Ahmadzaï

Madonna and Auto-Tune have had a long, not always healthy, and, at times, even toxic relationship. Although Madonna had committed to filtered vocals and dubs before, 'Nobody's Perfect' was a whole new pitch. Mirwais later pointed out 'Nobody's Perfect was 'the first track by a major star entirely sung on Auto-Tune' and based on his hit 'Naïve Song'. 'There's Auto-Tune all along,' he remarked. 'Madonna wanted it, so I wrote 'Nobody's Perfect' for her.' Presented during 2001's *Drowned World Tour*, it would be the only live outing for 'Nobody's Perfect', but there would be plenty more Auto-Tune to come.

'Don't Tell Me'

Maverick: 9 44910-2 **Single release:** November 2000 **Album:** *Music*
Writers: Madonna, Joe Henry, Mirwais Ahmadzaï
Producers: Madonna, Mirwais Ahmadzaï

Originally a Joe Henry song called 'Stop' he wrote in twenty-five minutes to keep himself busy, his wife (Melanie Ciccone) liked it so much she sent it to her sister. 'Don't Tell Me' has gone from being a great Madonna hit to her offhand reply to anyone ageist enough to dare question why she continues doing what she does. Peaking at #4 in both the US and UK, the folktronica 'Don't Tell Me' has since been sung on three of her tours and as a duet with Miley Cyrus. In 2005, jazz-pop singer Lizz Wright recorded the original 'Stop'.

Vid Bit!

Director: Jean-Baptiste Mondino

The fifth of the six Madonna/Mondino collabs, 'Don't Tell Me' was filmed just after Madonna gave birth to son Rocco. A tongue-in-cheek thrust at Western surreality, 'Don't Tell Me' made line dancing hip, cowboys sexy again and proved Madonna was still at the top of her game. 'Don't Tell Me' was nominated for a Grammy in 2002.

Remix Fix!

Thunderpuss, Richard 'Humpty' Vission, Victor Calderone, Tracy Young, and Timo Maas were all invited to the party. Newbie Dave Audé submitted remixes, rejected by Madonna's label, which have since appeared online.

'What It Feels Like for a Girl'

Maverick: 9362 42364-2 **Single release:** April 2001 **Album:** *Music*
Writers: Madonna, Guy Sigsworth, David Torn
Producers: Madonna, Guy Sigsworth, Mike "Spike" Stent

The third single from *Music* was inspired by the 1993 film *The Cement Garden*. Madonna was so taken with Charlotte Gainsbourg's dialogue she turned it into a song—'Secretly you'd love to know what it's like wouldn't you/ What it feels like for a girl'. Sigsworth had just co-produced *Empathy* from trip-hop duo Mandalay, one of Madonna's favourite records of the era. A #1 in Spain and a Top 10 single in the UK, 'What It Feels Like for a Girl' peaked at #23 in the US. A version was also recorded for the Latin market, 'Lo Que Siente La Mujer', with lyrics by Alberto Ferraras. Sigsworth later admitted 'WIFLFAG' sampled experimental musician David Torn from his 1987 album *Cloud About Mercury*. In 2010, during an episode of the *Glee* TV series, 'WIFLFAG' was sung by the male characters and released on the *Glee: The Music, The Power of Madonna* EP.

Vid Bit!

Director: Guy Ritchie

Madonna and Guy Ritchie on film, as in life it eventuated, were not a good match. The violent 'WIFLFAG' video became the first Madonna video since 'Erotica' to be banned by MTV. Ouch.

Remix Fix!

Above & Beyond's insistent trance mix, bravely omitting the bulk of the lyrics, was the version selected by Ritchie as the soundtrack to his wife's smash 'n' slab video. A long-overdue twelve-track package of 'What It Feels Like for a Girl' remixes was released digitally in April 2021.

'Gone'

Release: September 2000 **Album:** *Music*
Writers: Madonna, Damian LeGassick, Nik Young
Producers: Madonna, William Orbit, Mike "Spike" Stent

'Selling out is not my thing' begins the *Music* album closer with Madonna reverting to forlorn acoustic mode. The *Music* album, dubbed 'fresh' by *Spin*, 'radical' by *Q*, and 'a lick of pop genius' by *Mojo* was the ninth best-selling album of its year racking up healthy sales of 11 million worldwide. It was also Madonna's first US album topper since 1989's *Like a Prayer*. From five Grammy nominations *Music* won for Best Recording Package (with Mondino's cowgirl with ruby slippers photography). 'Gone', delivered with Madonna's vulnerable, impassioned vocals on 2001's Drowned World Tour, was afterwards gone for good.

'GHV2 Megamix'

Maverick: PRO-CD-100788 **Promo release:** November 2001
Songs: 'Don't Tell Me', 'Erotica', 'Secret', 'Frozen', 'What It Feels Like for a Girl', 'Take a Bow', 'Deeper and Deeper', 'Music', 'Ray of Light'
Remixers: Thunderpuss, Johnny Rocks & Mac Quayle, Tracy Young

Madonna's fourth compilation *GHV2*, aka 'Greatest Hits Volume 2', featured no new material, therefore her record company commissioned a batch of megamixes, stitching nine Madonna songs together, including ballad 'Take a Bow'. The Thunderpuss track clicked, reaching #5 in the US dance charts. Promo copies were given away with copies of *GHV2*, or later sold separately as collector's items.

VID BIT!

Director: Dago Gonzalez

Gonzalez curated Madonna's videography to match Thunderpuss's clever cut 'n' paste 'GHV2 Megamix'.

Dedicated to her father, Madonna's 1983 B&W self-titled debut album cover was taken by Australian Gary Heery. Originally titled *Lucky Star* for the album's first track (and later single) with different artwork, it was renamed as simply *Madonna*. In 1985, in the midst of 'Madonnamania', it was retitled, reshot (by George Holy), and rereleased as *The First Album*.

1984's *Like a Virgin* album was 'dedicated to the virgins of the world'. The cover was photographed by Steven Meisel, who would most famously (if not infamously) get into bed with Madonna again in 1992 on their racy little side project called *Sex*. 'Looking back it's hard to believe that this book caused so much controversy,' Madonna mused in 2020.

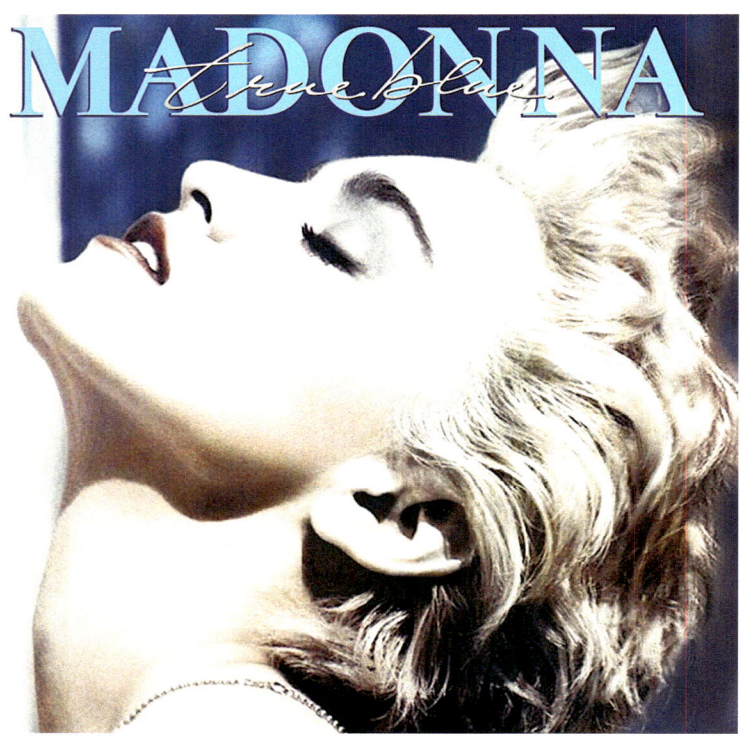

Madonna's third album, 1985's *True Blue*, was coolly and sexily photographed by Herb Ritts. Its blue-toned, hand-tinted, treated shot was ranked by *Billboard* magazine as one of the '50 Greatest Album Covers' in 2016. 'This album is dedicated to my husband, the coolest guy in the universe,' a truly loved-up Madonna penned on the album sleeve. Awww.

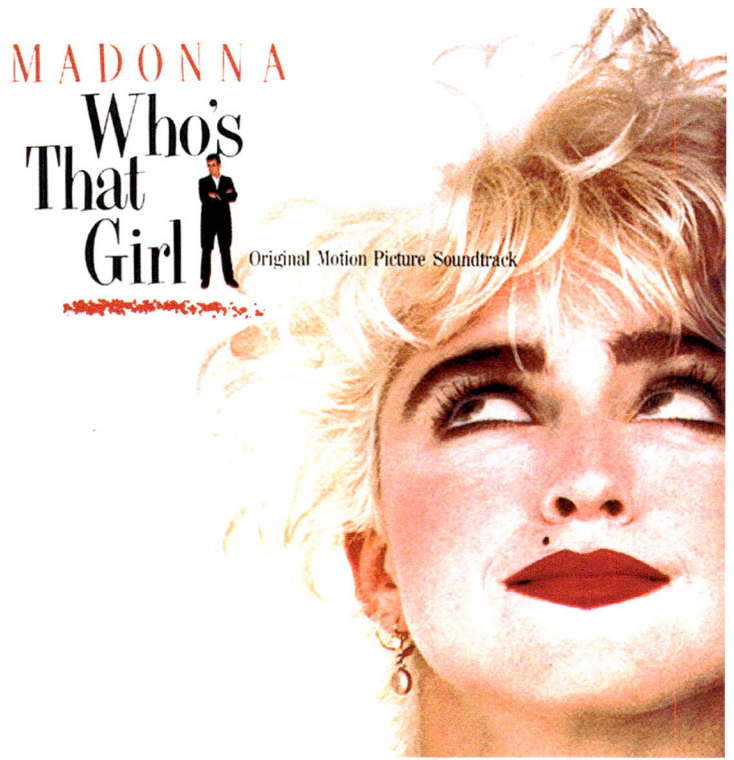

Madonna's 1987 soundtrack for her *Who's That Girl* movie repeated the same shot on the album cover as used on the movie poster. Madonna's four tracks (the title track, 'Causing a Commotion', 'The Look of Love' and 'Can't Stop') comprised less than half the album's brief thirty-seven-minute running time, but the soundtrack still swiftly sold over 6 million copies.

Once again featuring a cover shot by Herb Ritts, 1987's remix compilation *You Can Dance* possessed an extended essay by music journalist Brian Chin that profoundly pondered, 'Madonna and dancing. Madonna and dancers. Madonna and dance music. Madonna and dance music club disc jockers. These are four very special and ongoing love affairs.'

The first Madonna album cover not to feature her face, but her crotch instead, 1989's *Like a Prayer* also included some of Herb Ritts's most celebrated photography. 'This album is dedicated to my mother who taught me how to pray,' Madonna wrote on the sleeve alongside a heavenly B&W picture Ritts took of her in prayer mode (briefly sporting natural dark hair). Bless.

Above left: Not only was Madonna's brother, Christopher Ciccone, a dancer and artistic director (he was the genius behind 1990's *Blond Ambition*), but a painter too. Madonna admired his portrait of her so much (the falling 'P' refers to her divorce from Sean Penn) she made it the cover of her 'Like a Prayer' 12″ and Japanese *Remixed Prayers* eight-track mini-album.

Above right: 1990's 'Vogue' (pictured in its original 7″ UK picture disc) was written by Madonna with Shep Pettibone, who confessed she had 'actually seen voguing a long time ago in underground gay clubs and no one had really caught on to it. When she came in my studio she said, "I hope you don't mind, I'm going to call this song, *Vogue*." I thought it was *passé*!'

Fashion photographer Patrick Demarchelier snapped the cover of 1990's *I'm Breathless: Music From and Inspired by the Film Dick Tracy* album. On the sleeve Madonna thanked composer Stephen Sondheim 'for the privilege' and Warren Beatty (who on the front cover finally got to sit in the driver's set with her) 'for giving me the chance'. Neat!

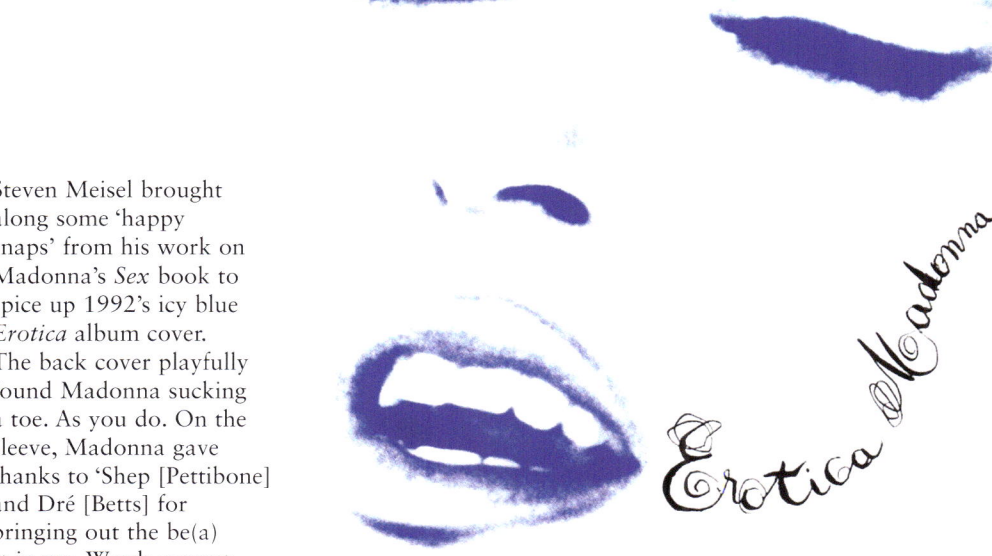

Emblazoned with logo art created by Warner Bros designer Jeri Heiden with husband, John Heiden, 1990's *The Immaculate Collection* compilation (dedicated to 'The Pope— my divine inspiration') showcased B&W sleeve photography by Herb Ritts. Having also directed her 1989 'Cherish' video, it was Ritts's final cover work for Madonna. He died of AIDS in 2002.

Steven Meisel brought along some 'happy snaps' from his work on Madonna's *Sex* book to spice up 1992's icy blue *Erotica* album cover. The back cover playfully found Madonna sucking a toe. As you do. On the sleeve, Madonna gave thanks to 'Shep [Pettibone] and Dré [Betts] for bringing out the be(a) st in me. Words cannot express. I'm unworthy!'

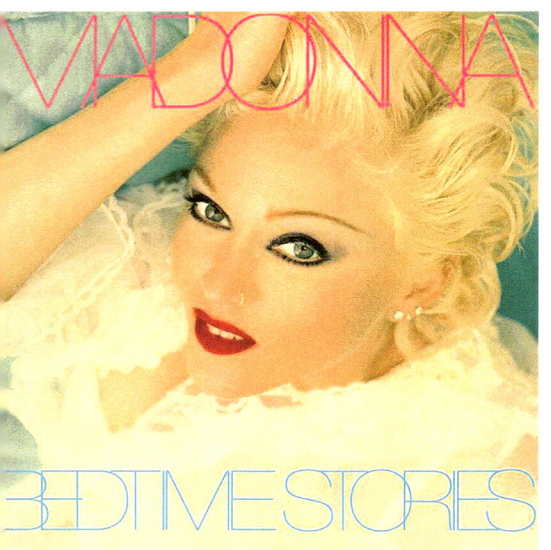 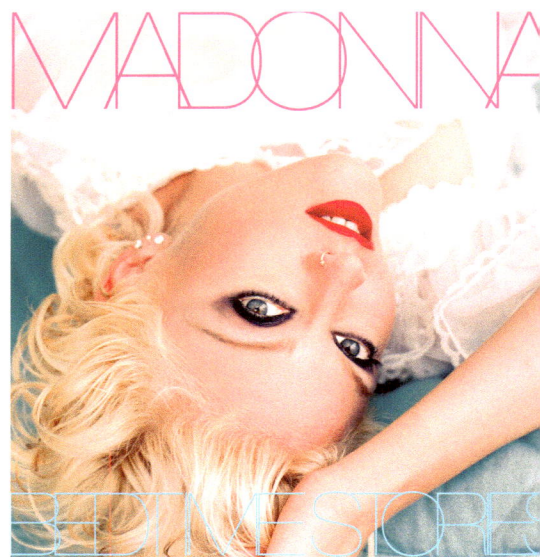

Above left: 1994's cosy and inviting *Bedtime Stories* album cover was by Patrick Demarchelier. During the production process the laidback shot was mistakenly printed with the photo upside down.

Above right: The 'correct' version of 1994's *Bedtime Stories* album cover (Madonna lying down) which appeared on later editions, although the 'incorrect' cover has become the default standard.

Below: One of the rarest (and most precious) of all Madonna releases is 1995's UK 'Bedtime Story' CD single with a luscious fourteen-page bedtime storybook of the lyrics illustrated by Mark Bannerman. The release contained Junior Vasquez's single remix and three mixes of 'Secret'. The second disc (sold separately) boasted five mixes and edits of 'Bedtime Story'. The end.

MADONNA

SOMETHING TO REMEMBER

Above: For the cover of 1995's ballads compilation, *Something to Remember*, Madonna chose Mario Testino, soon after to famously photographed Princess Diana before her untimely death. Madonna wrote on the album sleeve, 'while I have no regrets regarding the choices I've made artistically, I've learned to appreciate the idea of doing things in a simpler way'.

Below: Two versions of the *Evita* soundtrack, both photographed by David Appleby, were released in 1996. A double-disc 'motion picture music soundtrack' and a single disc 'music from the motion picture' with co-star Antonio Banderas also appearing on the cover. Madonna thanked vocal coach Joan Lader on both albums 'for helping me find my voice'.

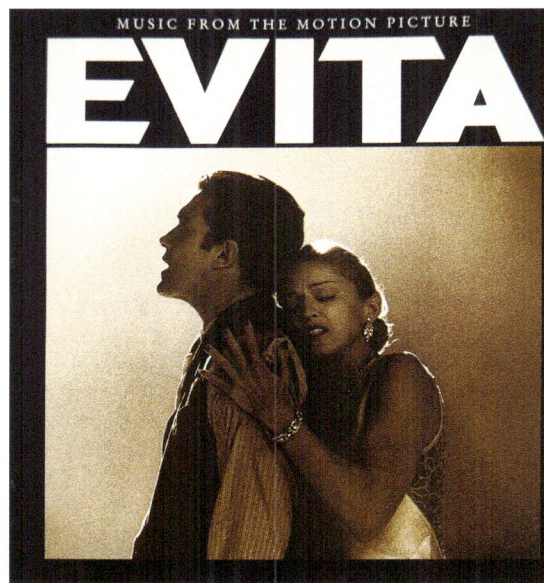

Mario Testino returned to capture the wistful, windswept cover for 1998's *Ray of Light* album. After thanking a number of people on the album sleeve for 'creative and spiritual guidance', Madonna gave special thanks to this classic album's main producer 'Billy Bubbles aka William Orbit for sharing my vision and daring to dream. Awright geez, sorted, init'.

The soundtrack for Madonna's 2000 movie co-starring Rupert Everett, *The Next Best Thing*, starred the crowd-dividing 'American Pie' (with Everett on backing vocals) and the underrated 'Time Stood Still'. The cover was photographed by Dah Len, while Madonna was credited as album executive producer having personally selected the songs.

Director of six Madonna videos (including that album's 'Don't Tell Me'), French auteur Jean-Baptiste Mondino was also responsible for the cover of 2000's *Music*. The album design by art director Kevin Reagan was so inspired (iconic Madonna + Americana = cool cowgirl!) it won a Grammy the following year for Best Recording Package.

Peer closely at the cover of Madonna's 2001 *GHV2* by Regan Cameron and you will see—spotted!—the album's minimalist title reflected in her eye. The inside sleeve was littered with hundreds of Madonna pictures, some stretching much further back than the 1992–2000 period this compilation covered, including 'True Blue', 'La Isla Bonita', and 'Into the Groove'.

In lieu of a new single, 2001's 'Thunderpuss GHV2 Megamix' was widely used for the marketing of Madonna's *GHV2* compilation that same year. The promo CD single—which was sold in some territories—contained two different edits, plus the original 4:50 version. The Thunderpuss remix duo, Chris Cox and Barry Harris, disbanded two years later.

Reinventing herself as a rock revolutionary in the style of Che Guevera on the cover of 2003's *American Life* album (photographed by Craig McDean), Madonna proved she was more a traditional wife in the sleeve notes gushing, 'and the most special thanks to my mister for shining his light in my direction.' It was, also, printed on 100 per cent recycled paper. Phew.

Released just six months after *American Life*, 2003's *Remixed & Revisited* 'rock and retro' EP at under thirty minutes accommodated seven tracks (one being the MTV performance of 'Like a Virgin/ Hollywood Medley' with Britney Spears, Christina Aguilera, and Missy Elliott). The cover, by Regan Cameron, is also the only Madonna release to feature aliens. Possibly.

Steven Klein made his first appearance for a Madonna album cover snapping a supple, red-haired, pink-leotarded Queen of Pop for 2005's *Confessions on a Dance Floor*. Besides thanking ABBA in the credits, Madonna gave 'extra special thanks to the Thin White Duke aka Stuart Price—without you this record never would have happened'.

For his second act, Steven Klein got to photograph Madonna in fighting mode on the cover of 2008's *Hard Candy*. Besides thanking her producers/new besties Justin Timberlake, Pharrell Williams, and Timbaland, Madonna cryptically sent a message to her new manager Guy Oseary in the sleeve notes teasing, 'thanks to Guy O—be careful what you wish for'.

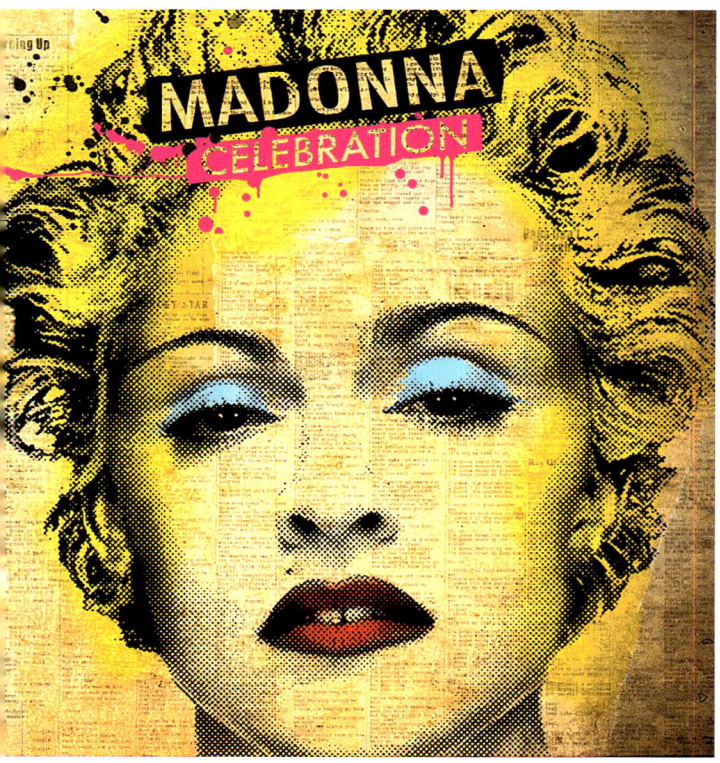

2009's *Celebration* compilation (released as both a thirty-six-track double CD and eighteen-track single disc) featured artwork by maverick Mr Brainwash. He created fifteen different versions, making it an expensive celebration for Madonna completists. Just like *The Immaculate Collection* some nineteen years earlier, *Celebration* debuted two new songs—the title track and 'Revolver'.

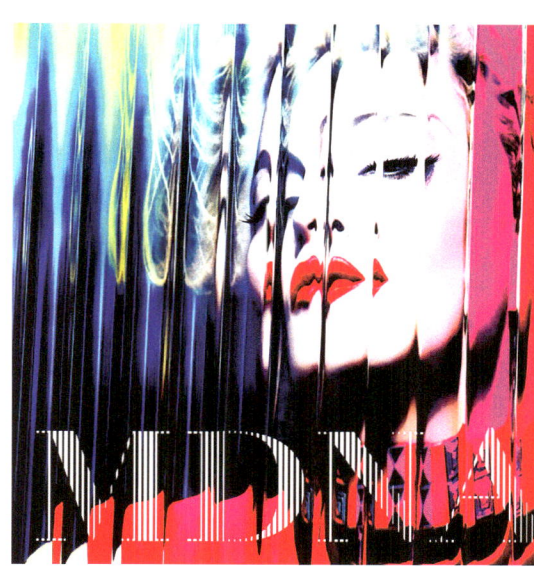

Above left: 2012's *MDNA* twelve-track standard edition album cover was shot by Mert Alaş and Marcus Piggott. Madonna gave mystifying thanks on the sleeve to mixer Demacio Castellon for 'turning up the heat & putting out the fires!'

Above right: 2012's *MDNA* Deluxe Edition, with a slightly tweaked cover, added four new songs ('Beautiful Killer', 'I Fucked Up', 'B-Day Song', and 'Best Friend'), plus a bonus Party Rock Remix of 'Give Me All Your Luvin".

Below: Why have one, or two, versions of your album when you can have three? 2015's *Rebel Heart* offered a standard edition fourteen-track album (cover pictured), deluxe nineteen-track version, and a twenty-five-track super deluxe edition. All three were again photographed by Mert & Marcus.

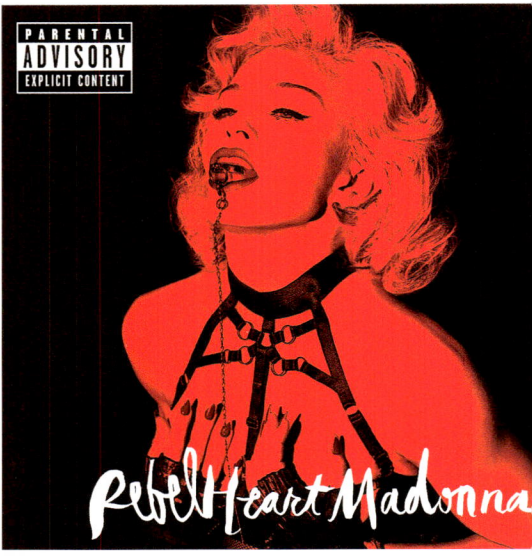

Above left: The B&W 'tangled life of Madonna' *Rebel Heart* cover, which lived for love on the deluxe edition, was deemed the regulation album cover for the project. The deluxe album added five songs ('Best Night', 'Veni Vidi Vici', 'S.E.X.', 'Messiah', and the title track).

Above right: The super deluxe edition cover of *Rebel Heart* seemed like a throwback to 1992's *Erotica*. Besides two remixes of 'Living for Love', four more songs were added ('Beautiful Scars', 'Borrowed Time', 'Addicted', and 'Graffiti Heart'). 'Queen' was cut at the last moment.

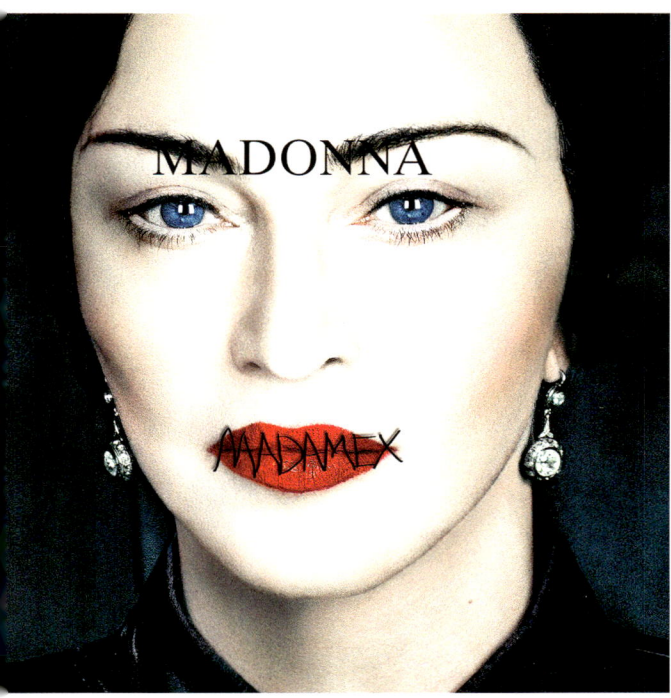

Repeating the 'triple release' album strategy for 2019's *Madame X*, shoppers could select from a thirteen-track standard edition (with its tight-lipped, Frida Kahlo-inspired cover), fifteen-track deluxe edition (Soviet realism chic), or eighteen-track deluxe boxset (two discs, one guitarist).

Above: The deluxe edition of *Madame X* added two songs—the masterful 'Extreme Occident' and the divine ballad 'Looking for Mercy'. Just as Madonna had reconnected with Mirwais for the bulk of the album's music, she reunited with Steven Klein for the *Madame X* artwork.

Right: Adding an extra disc of three new songs ('Funana', 'Back That Up to the Beat', and 'Ciao Bella'), the deluxe two-disc edition of *Madame X* pictured Madonna holding a guitar on the cover and—arguably less shockingly—holding her crotch inside.

MADAME X

Dua Lipa's 2020 *Club Future Nostalgia* remix album not only featured the uplifting 'Levitating' with Madonna, but awarded her a guest spot on its cover collage. The other artists surrounding hung up dancing queen Lipa were (*left to right*) Missy Elliott, Mark Ronson, Gwen Stefani, and The Blessed Madonna.

15

The *American Life/Remixed &*
Revisited Era

American Life
Maverick: 48439-2
Released: April 2003
Tracklist

'American Life'	4:57
'Hollywood'	4:24
'I'm So Stupid'	4:08
'Love Profusion'	3:37
'Nobody Knows Me'	4:39
'Nothing Fails'	4:48
'Intervention'	4:54
'X-Static Process'	3:49
'Mother and Father'	4:33
'Die Another Day'	4:38
'Easy Ride'	5:05

Remixed & Revisited EP
Maverick: 9362-48624-2
Released: November 2003
Tracklist

'Nothing Fails' (Nevins Mix)	3:50
'Love Profusion' (Headcleanr Rock Mix)	3:16
'Nobody Knows Me' (Mount Sims Old School Mix)	4:44
'American Life' (Headcleanr Rock Mix)	4:01
'Like a Virgin/Hollywood Medley' (2003 MTV VMA Performance)	5:34
'Into the Hollywood Groove' (The Passengerz Mix)	3:42
'Your Honesty'	4:07

'Die Another Day'

Warner Bros. Records: 42492-2 **Single release:** October 2002 **Soundtrack:** *Die Another Day* **Album:** *American Life*
Writers/Producers: Madonna, Mirwais Ahmadzaï

Madonna and Mirwais concocted an angry, bristling electroclash-with-strings title song for the twentieth 007 movie. Madonna also landed herself a minor role as a wise-quipping fencing seductress called Verity ('I see you handle your weapon well!'). 'Die Another Day' returned Madonna to #8 in the US and #3 in the UK, earned a Golden Globe nomination, two Grammy nominations and ushered her into the record books as the artist with the then most Top 40 singles in the US (44), besting Queen of Soul, Aretha Franklin. Elton John, however, mocked it as 'the worst Bond tune ever' leading to an ongoing feud between the two divas.

VID BIT!
Director: Traktor

If you thought 'What It Feels Like for a Girl' was an exercise in violent behaviour, then 'Die Another Day' took it to the next level. Thanks to some deft special effects, Madonna was reimaged as a fencing vixen fighting herself, ranking as the second most expensive video of all time ($6.1 million) behind Michael and Janet Jackson's 1995 'Scream'.

REMIX FIX!
Felix Da Housecat's on point Thee RetroLectro Mix turned things even angrier, nastier and riskier, while Tiësto's Dedicated Remix rebirthed 'DAD' on another level all together.

'American Life'

Maverick: 16658-2 **Single release:** April 2003 **Album:** *American Life*
Writers/Producers: Madonna, Mirwais Ahmadzaï

American Life is undoubtedly Madonna's riskiest album sonically, lyrically and politically. The song 'American Life' itself spluttered further into innovative, lo-fi Euro-techno complete with relentless Auto-Tuned vocals. *Nouveau* 'British' Madonna preached, and even rapped, about life, love, and lattes. Although filmed long before the Iraqi war commenced, the apocalyptic 'American Life' video was released in the middle of the Iraqi combat operation. A subsequent desert shitstorm blew up in the media and Madonna was caught dead centre. The single reached #2 in the UK, but stalled at #37 in the US. Shifting just 5 million copies, *American Life* tallied as Madonna's worst selling studio album to date. Although she performed the title song during her 2004 Re-Invention World Tour (filmed for 2005's *I'm Going to Tell You a Secret* doco) it was not until her Madame X 2019–2020 Tour 'American Life' returned to prominence, given an overdue favourable critical reappraisal.

VID BIT!
Director: Jonas Åkerlund

The dark, hyper-political and traumatic first 'American Life' video savaged both war and the fashion industry ('Fashion Victim') and made fun of then US President George W. Bush. Quickly withdrawn due to the Gulf War, a blander, chaste video of Madonna singing in front of world flags was summoned.

REMIX FIX!
Peter Rauhofer and his American Anthem (Part 1 and Part 2, adding up to twenty minutes) transformed 'American Life' into a global club hymn, with Madonna's rap rant spat out at the end.

'Hollywood'

Maverick: 42638-2 **Single release:** July 2003 **Album:** *American Life*
Writers/Producers: Madonna, Mirwais Ahmadzaï

The second single from the *American Life* album was a whirling dervish of an acoustic-electro readymade pop smash. While the UK was receptive to 'Hollywood', hitting #2, the song failed to enter the US Top 100. Yet when *Rolling Stone* reassessed Madonna's 50 Greatest Songs in 2015 they ranked 'Hollywood' at #44. A victim of bad timing and bad blood, 'Hollywood' deserved much better.

VID BIT!
Director: Jean-Baptiste Mondino

His sixth and final video for Madonna, Mondino was interested in presenting the 'artifice that Hollywood can provide'. As its title suggested, this Madonna single was all about old-school screen queen glamour, but with a twist, if not a botox needle or two. Inspired by the photographs of French fashion snapper Guy Bourdin (who died in 1991), his family sued Madonna over the similarities in Mondino's 'Hollywood' video, reaching a financial settlement thought to be $600,000. The 'Hollywood' video was, however, cast in the shade by Madonna's performance of the song as the opening number on the *MTV Video Music Awards* where she kissed both Britney Spears and Christina Aguilera and they liked it.

Remix Fix!

Jacques Lu Cont's Thin White Duke Mix! JLC was one of the many pseudonyms Stuart Price gave himself. Pointing to where Madonna would head next, his glitzy slither of flashy disco-house on 'Hollywood' led to Price producing her next album.

'I'm So Stupid'

Release: April 2003 **Album:** *American Life*
Writers/Producers: Madonna, Mirwais Ahmadzaï, Mark 'Spike' Stent

'Cos I used to live/In a fuzzy dream' begins another of a stream of virtually anti-pop songs on *American Life*. Radically mixing indie rock guitars with minimalist electronica, 'I'm So Stupid' revelled in its deployment of Auto-Tune on Madonna's vocals. An open evaluation of greed, celebrity and her own perceived stupidity ('I was stupid/Stupider than stupid') this is Madonna taking a good hard look at her privileged life as a celebrity and breaking it down to see that there needs to be more, or else her dreams will not add up to anything, if nothing at all. Madonna's affection for this misfit from her back catalogue is quite apparent as it was one of four songs from *American Life* she performed during her two-off *Tears of a Clown* shows in Melbourne and Miami in 2016.

'Love Profusion'

Maverick: 9362 42692 2 **Single release:** December 2003 **Album:** *American Life*
Writers/Producers: Madonna, Mirwais Ahmadzaï

If 'I Deserve It' was Madonna's love song dedication to new husband Guy Ritchie on the *Music* album, then 'Love Profusion' continued the bad romance on *American Life*. Sadly, there wasn't enough love for 'Love Profusion' when released as a single, becoming Madonna's second single in a row to miss the US Top 100, due to an utter lack of radio support. It also just missed the UK top 10 at #11, her first to do so since 1996's 'One More Chance'. Completely swamped, if not engulfed, in the wash up from the *American Life* storm aftermath, *Entertainment Weekly* magazine bravely described 'Love Profusion' as 'one of Madonna's finest folktronica moments'.

Vid Bit!

Director: Luc Besson

'I always have a lot of fairies dancing around me,' Madonna quipped tongue-in-cheek about this fairy-tale special effects video, although to be fair Madonna does a lot more walking here than actual dancing.

Remix Fix!

Ralphi Rosario, Headcleanr, Passengerz, Blow-Up, Craig J and Peter Rauhofer all responded for remix duty.

'Nobody Knows Me'

Single release: October 2003 (B-side of 'Nothing Fails') **Album:** *American Life*
Writers/Producers: Madonna, Mirwais Ahmadzaï

A virtual double A-side with 'Nothing Fails' when released as a single in October 2003, both it and 'Nobody Knows Me' suffered, not due to quality issues, but because there were no video for either track released—the first for a Madonna single since 'Rescue Me' in 1991. With its heavy use of vocoder effects, bubbling electronic backing, and vehemently critical lyrics, 'Nobody Knows Me' was Madonna once more in angry, anti-pop mode. Almost a decade later, 'Nobody Knows Me' became a moving interlude on 2012's *MDNA* featuring Madonna photographs coming to life lip-syncing the lyrics as images and names of teenagers who have died from anti-gay bullying appeared. Controversial far-right French politician Marine Le Pen threatened to sue Madonna for using her face morphing into a swastika and Hitler's face during the 'Nobody Knows Me' video interlude. During the French concerts Madonna switched the swastika to a question mark, declaring, 'I know that I made a certain Marine Le Pen very angry with me. And it's not my intention to make enemies.'

Remix Fix!

'Nobody Knows Me' reached a respectable #4 on the US Dance Club Songs chart and also just made the Australian dance charts, though due to its length was not eligible for the singles chart.

'Nothing Fails'

Maverick: 42682-2 **Single release:** October 2003 **Album:** *American Life*
Writers: Madonna, Guy Sigsworth, Jem Griffiths
Producers: Madonna, Mirwais Ahmadzaï, Mark "Spike" Stent

Welsh singer/songwriter Griffiths originally wrote 'Nothing Fails' with producer Sigworth. 'When I finally heard the finished song, it was the strangest experience,' Griffiths related. 'It's not every day you hear Madonna singing words and melodies you sang into your Dictaphone at two in the morning!' With its soaring gospel choir reminiscent of 1989's 'Like a Prayer' (courtesy of the London Community Gospel Choir) and Madonna in gentler mode singing a naïve and honest love song, 'Nothing Fails' should have flourished. Instead, with no video, a virtual US radio blackban, not to mention having to compete simultaneously with Madonna's duet with Britney Spears, 'Me Against the Music', it failed to crack the US Top 100. The UK gave the 'Nothing Fails' single a #11 peak, however, while it was another #1 in Spain. In 2012, Griffiths's demo of 'Nothing Fails' leaked under its original title 'Silly Thing'.

Remix Fix!
'Nothing Fails' was another #1 on the US Dance Club Song chart, thanks to remixes from Jason Nevins, Tracy Young, Peter Rauhofer and Jackie Christie.

'Intervention'

Release: April 2003 **Album:** *American Life*
Writers/Producers: Madonna, Mirwais Ahmadzaï

A somewhat underrated, if neglected, rock-electronica fusion album track on its initial release, 'Intervention' took on a truly heartbreaking poignancy when Madonna dedicated it to her son, Rocco, during her Melbourne *Tears of a Clown* show in 2016. In the midst of a custody battle with ex-husband Guy Ritchie, images of Rocco appeared on the screen behind her as his obviously anguished mother sang, 'I got to save my baby because he makes me cry/I got to make him happy I got to teach him how to fly'. The matter would mercifully be resolved, however, and the following year Madonna adopted Malawi twins Estere and Stella.

'X-Static Process'

Release: April 2003 **Album:** *American Life*
Writers: Madonna, Stuart Price
Producers: Madonna, Mirwais Ahmadzaï

After having becoming musical director for Madonna's Drowned World Tour, Price remixed a number of her songs and co-wrote 'X-Static Process'. This reflective, mostly acoustic ballad ruminates on managing a relationship with a handsome, gifted husband. Uh-huh. Madonna played 'X-Static Process' twice in 2003—on her MTV special and during her Paris promo show. 'It started off being a love song, but then the subject of Jesus crept in and I realised that my problem with men is the same as my problem with Jesus,' she explained, 'if you give Jesus/men more power than they deserve then you will get fucked.' Madonna later performed 'X-Static Process' during her 2016 *Tears of a Clown* concert, taking on a new poignancy in the wake of her custody battle.

'Mother and Father'

Release: April 2003 **Album:** *American Life*
Writers/Producers: Madonna, Mirwais Ahmadzaï

'Mother and Father' is one of the most affecting tracks on *American Life* as Madonna engages in some on-record therapy, resulting in her finally accepting her own father was traumatized by his wife's death too. On 2004's Re-Invention World Tour, complete with excerpts from *Intervention*, Madonna sang 'Mother and Father' against a backdrop of a heart and Jesus on the cross before they dissolve as she has 'got to give it up and find somebody else'. For the Chicago concert stop, Madonna's father and stepmother were shown supportively singing and dancing along to 'Mother and Father', documented in 2005 *I'm Going to Tell You a Secret*.

REMIX FIX!
Peter Rauhofer's 'Mother and Father' pounding Re-Invention Mix, one of his most sought-after Madonna remixes, was promoed on Star 69 Records (his boutique label) and released on 2004's *Peter Rauhofer Live @ Roxy 4* album.

'Easy Ride'

Release: April 2003 **Album:** *American Life*
Writers: Madonna, Monte Pittman
Producers: Madonna, Mirwais Ahmadzaï

The closing track on the *American Life* album is a sombre, restrained ballad, that half-way through becomes a regulation Mirwais production with more chopped-up strings evoking 'Die Another Day'. 'Easy Ride' was written by Madonna and Pittman, the man who taught her, and Guy Ritchie, how to play guitar. After working as a guitar store salesman in LA, he turned to teaching, with his third student being Ritchie, who had been given a guitar as a present by then girlfriend Madonna. Ritchie bought Madonna a guitar and she too began lessons with Pittman. Soon after he was working with Madonna on stage and has played in her band during all her subsequent concerts and live shows right up to 2019–2020's *Madame X*. Madonna performed 'Easy Ride' during her 2016 *Tears of a Clown* show in Melbourne, where she shared her love life philosophy of always saying, 'Sorry, you're right!'

REMIX FIX!
Tracy Young and Giangi Cappai's stabbing remix of 'Easy Ride' featured exclusively on Young's 2005 *Danceculture* album.

'Me Against the Music' (Britney Spears Featuring Madonna)

Jive: 82876-58212-2 **Single release:** October 2003 **Album:** *In the Zone*
Writers: Britney Spears, Madonna, Christopher 'Tricky' Stewart, Thabiso 'Tab' Nikhereanye, Penelope Magnet, Terius Nash, Gary O'Bryan
Producers: Trixster, Penelope Magnet

'Me Against the Music' was the lead single from Britney Spears' fourth album, *In the Zone*, released in October 2003 in the midst of the *American Life* backlash. Spears had played Madonna the track during rehearsals for their infamous *MTV Music Video Awards* smooch in August and the two agreed to release it as duet, if not a musical/love battle. In the US the single only managed a #35 peak, though 'Me Against the Music' was a chart topper in Australia, Spain, and reached #2 in the UK.

VID BIT!

Director: Paul Hunter

After a kind of 'cat and mouse foreplay' Hunter had his two female leads literally chase each other around for the duration of the song before Madonna disappeared in a puff of smoke at the end. In 2003, *French & Saunders* hilariously parodied the clip on their BBC series, while the 2010 *Glee* series episode *Britney/Brittany* had Heather Morris as Britney/Brittany and Naya Rivera as Santana/Madonna—plus a cameo from the real Britney!—which also briefly charted in some territories. Rivera, tragically, drowned in a lake accident in 2020.

REMIX FIX!

Rishi Rish's Desi Kulcha Remix successfully took the song into an unexpectedly exotic Eastern direction, while a still relatively unknown Kanye West added urban verve to his remix.

'Your Honesty'

Release: November 2003 **Compilation:** *Remixed & Revisited*
Writers/Producers: Madonna, Dallas Austin

Ransacking her annals for 2003's rocky, mostly unlistenable *Remixed & Revisited* EP, Madonna's then manager Caresse Henry dredged up 'Your Honesty', though it actually fell off 1994's *Bedtime Stories*. Although its 1990s R&B groove arrived a decade too late, the song incorporates a smoochy French spoken word interlude. Henry and Madonna would part ways soon after this was released. Tragically Henry committed suicide in 2010.

16

The *Confessions on a Dance Floor* Era

Confessions on a Dance Floor
Warner Bros. Records: 49460-2
Released: November 2005
Tracklist

'Hung Up'	5:36
'Get Together'	5:30
'Sorry'	4:44
'Future Lovers'	4:51
'I Love New York'	4:11
'Let It Will Be'	4:18
'Forbidden Love'	4:22
'Jump'	3:47
'How High'	4:40
'Isaac'	6:04
'Push'	3:57
'Like it or Not'	4:32

Limited Edition Bonus Track

'Fighting Spirit'	3:32

Icon Members Bonus Track

'Super Pop'	3:42

'Hung Up'

Warner Bros. Records: 42845-2 **Single release:** October 2005 **Album:** *Confessions on a Dance Floor*
Writers: Madonna, Stuart Price, Benny Andersson, Björn Ulvaeus
Producers: Madonna, Stuart Price

Planning to work predominantly with Mirwais on her tenth studio album, after getting together with Price for one track, Team Madonna judiciously decided this should dictate the direction for her new album. That song, the album's first single, was 'Hung Up', which did not so much as sample ABBA's 1979 disco era hit 'Gimme! Gimme! Gimme! (A Man After Midnight)' as ingeniously morph it into a post-modern, post-disco masterpiece. 'She asked us so nicely,' the band's Andersson admitted. 'It was a great record so we said, "Yeah, sure, fine. You could use it, but we split the copyright!"' Upon release 'Hung Up' and accompanying retro-disco album, *Confessions on a Dance Floor*, sold in huge quantities, glitterbombing the globe via its mirror ball omnipotence. Despite a vox-less version leaking prior to release, 'Hung Up' hit #1 in forty-one countries and was also immensely successful as a ringtone. Though reaching only #7 in the US due to lack of radio support, the single sold over 9 million copies worldwide. Twenty years into her career, 'Hung Up' flawlessly reminded the world Madonna was still their favourite dancing queen.

Vid Bit!

Director: Johan Renck

Influenced by David LaChapelle's *Rize* documentary about the krumping dance style, LaChapelle pulled out of Madonna's 'Hung Up' video due to 'creative differences', but Madonna still employed some of his film's dancers. A few weeks prior to filming Madonna fell off her horse, breaking eight bones, but despite the pain persevered with the shoot. In 2020, *Billboard* ranked the glorious 'Hung Up' #79 on its list of 100 greatest music videos of the twenty-first century.

Remix Fix!

Having Madonna and ABBA on the one record was already perfect enough, certainly for her gay audience. Only extending every little thing Madonna sang, or did, on 'Hung Up' could improve it. Thankfully SDP (Stuart David Price using his initials) thought the same, elongating the original from five minutes to almost eight.

'Get Together'

Warner Bros. Records: 42935-2 **Single release:** June 2006 **Album:** *Confessions on a Dance Floor*
Writers: Madonna, Stuart Price, Anders Bagge, Peer Åström
Producers: Madonna, Stuart Price

Confessions on a Dance Floor was not an album hung up on one great single. There were four great singles and just as many great non-singles. 'Get Together' was the third single and a feisty rewrite of Stardust's 1998 'Music Sounds Better With You' hit, itself based on a sample from Chaka Khan's 1981 song 'Fate'. The Balearic bliss of 'Get Together' hit #7 in the UK, #1 in Spain, Hungary, and Venezuela, and #13 in Australia. Again, due to lack of radio support, it failed to chart on the Hot 100 in the US, but was nominated for a Grammy for Best Dance Recording, alas losing to Justin Timberlake's 'SexyBack'. Although performed during promotional gigs for the album and then on the 2006 Confessions Tour these would be the only live outings for *Get Together*. A dramatically different demo version of 'Get Together', more closely related to Donna Summer's 'I Feel Love', leaked in 2010.

VID BIT!

Director: Logan Studios

Mixing animation by 2D/3D artist Nathaniel Howe with Madonna's performance of the song at London's Koko Club in late 2005, the original trancey if pretty spacey 'Get Together' clip was reworked for the US market into more of a performance/dance animation targeted at clubs. The director for the alternate 'Get Together' was Eugene Riecansky.

REMIX FIX!

With Stuart Price now not just one of the world's most in-demand producers but remixers (winning his first Grammy in 2004 for remixing No Doubt's 'It's My Life') who better to twiddle the knobs on 'Get Together'? Price would garner another Grammy in 2007 for Best Electronic/Dance Album for *Confessions on a Dance Floor*.

'Sorry'

Warner Bros. Records: 42892-2 **Single release:** February 2006 **Album:** *Confessions on a Dance Floor*

Writers/Producers: Madonna, Stuart Price

Much of the lyrical ideas and content for the *Confessions* era songs came from two musicals Madonna had been working on then scrapped. One was called *Hello Suckers* and the other, not titled, was to be produced with Luc Besson about a woman on her deathbed, looking back on her life, with disco songs Madonna insisted sounded like 'ABBA on drugs'. 'Sorry' surely fits that description. On the album's second single Madonna says 'Sorry' in ten languages (though perplexingly not in German) helping it become her twelfth #1 in the UK, according her a new chart record of the female artist with the most #1s. 'Sorry' also enjoyed Top 5 status around the globe, but again, the US resisted its irresistible charms languishing at #58. Some 5,000 Madonna fans signed a petition to end what they considered a radio boycott of Madonna in the US by Clear Channel, now iHeartMedia, the biggest owner of radio stations in the US. The company, with strong ties to the Republican Party, had 'no comment', nor did they say sorry.

VID BIT!
Director: Jamie King

Madonna choreographer King took over the directing reins for a glittery blur of disco dancing, rollerskating, more leotards and Madonna's roaming 'Pimp My Ride' van.

REMIX FIX!
Pet Shop Boys' Maxi Mix, featuring additional vocals from the band's Neil Tennant, caught on big and Madonna employed this version on 2006's Confessions Tour.

'Future Lovers'

Release: November 2005 **Album:** *Confessions on a Dance Floor*
Writers/Producers: Madonna, Mirwais Ahmadzaï

'Future Lovers' was the third song written for the *Confessions* album, after 'Hung Up' and 'Sorry', but Madonna's first with Mirwais. While it is easy to see why Madonna responded to Price's relentlessly upbeat 'let's go disco' call, the two Mirwais contributions ('Let It Will Be' being the other) gave the album some balance and depth it might otherwise have lacked. 'Future Lovers' truly came to life as the opening number of Madonna's 2006 Confessions Tour fused together with one of the songs it celebrates, Donna Summer and Giorgio Moroder's classic 1977 disco hit 'I Feel Love'. Cutting edge *Vice* magazine later ranked *Confessions* as the third best dance album of all time.

'I Love New York'

Release: November 2005 **Album:** *Confessions on a Dance Floor*
Writers/Producers: Madonna, Stuart Price

Already given an airing during 2005's *I'm Going to Tell You a Secret* doco (and 2006 CD version in its original hard rock demo version), 'I Love New York' was proof Madonna had not gone completely apolitical. Although Madonna was by this stage living in London, in 'ILNY' she trashes her new hometown, as well as Los Angeles and Paris for the joys of the Big Apple. For the filmed show of 2006's Confessions Tour Madonna changed the lyrics from 'Just go to Texas that's where they golf' to 'Just go to Texas and you can suck George Bush's dick'. What's not to love?

REMIX FIX!
In April 2006, a limited triple vinyl *Confessions Remixed* album, with six Price remixes including his reheated Thin White Duke Mix of 'I Love New York' (later added to the single release of 'Get Together'), was issued.

'Let It Will Be'

Release: November 2005 **Album:** *Confessions on a Dance Floor*
Writers: Madonna, Mirwais Ahmadzaï, Stuart Price
Producers: Madonna, Stuart Price

Taking a further swipe at success and fame on the second Mirwais track on *Confessions,* this time he shared a co-writing credit. 'Now I can see things for what they really are/I guess I'm not that far I'm at the point of no return' suggests Madonna putting to bed any grievances she held over her past treatment in the public eye. Price, via his Paper Faces moniker, remixed 'Let It Will Be' into a seven-and-a-half minute stomping epic that appeared as the B-side on the 'Sorry' single. This was also the version Madonna performed on 2006's Confessions Tour. A more low-key demo of the Mirwais version of 'Let It Will Be' leaked in 2011.

'Forbidden Love'

Release: November 2005 **Album:** *Confessions on a Dance Floor*
Writers/Producers: Madonna, Stuart Price

This 'Forbidden Love' is not to be confused with Babyface's lush ballad 'Forbidden Love' from 1994's *Bedtime Stories*, though Madonna would not mind if you did. 'I did all of that on purpose,' she grinned in an interview. 'I mean, if I'm going to plagiarize somebody, it might as well be me, right?' When staged live on 2006's Confessions Tour this 'Forbidden Love' denoted a defiant cry for coexistence featuring a male dancer with a Jewish star of David and another male dancer with an Islamic moon pulling at each other before finally hugging. Towards the end of the performance Madonna dances with another star/moon couple, ensuring the Confessions Tour version of 'Forbidden Love' became another iconic gay Madonna moment.

'Jump'

Warner Bros. Records: 42978-2 **Single release:** October 2006 **Album:** *Confessions on a Dance Floor*
Writers: Madonna, Joe Henry, Stuart Price
Producers: Madonna, Stuart Price

In 2020, Pet Shop Boys told this author 'on Madonna's *Confessions on a Dance Floor* there's a song where Stuart sampled "West End Girls"'. Is it 'Jump'? It may well be and much of the fun of *Confessions* is trying to spot the samples, or tributes, to disco era heroes like the Bee Gees, Cerrone, and Giorgio Moroder/ Donna Summer among others. The joy-affirming, forward-thinking, fourth and final *Confessions* single, 'Jump' was another co-write with her brother-in-law Henry with his customary wordplay twists. A #1 hit in Italy and Hungary, and #9 in the UK, 'Jump' again failed to make the US Top 100. Performed during the 'equine' opening section of 2006's Confessions Tour with her dancers 'Jump' provided some impressive parkour leaps.

VID BIT!

Director: Jonas Åkerlund

One of Madonna's most literal music video translations of her lyrics, there is plenty of jumping in the 'Jump' video, filmed in Tokyo by Åkerlund on a day off from the Confessions Tour.

REMIX FIX!

Price delivered a drama-tinged Jacques Lu Cont mix of 'Jump', while Junior Sanchez added an indie electro flavour to the original, yet it was the swirling Scandi-dance Axwell Remix that got the jump on the competition.

'How High'

Release: November 2005 **Album:** *Confessions on a Dance Floor*
Writers: Madonna, Christian Karlsson, Pontus Winnberg, Henrik Jonback
Producers: Madonna, Bloodshy & Avant, Stuart Price

'I spent my whole life wanting to be talked about!' found Madonna again self-reflecting on her prominent place in the world. Another of Madonna's early stabs at EDM, 'How High' helped *Confessions on a Dance Floor* sell over 10 million copies worldwide becoming the thirty-second best-selling album of the noughties. *NME* awarded it 9/10, *Entertainment Weekly* a B+, and *Q* magazine four out of five stars. Karlsson and Winnberg were Swedish songwriting producer duo Bloodshy & Avant whose big moment came co-writing/producing 'Toxic' for Britney Spears, winning a Grammy in 2005 for Best Dance Recording.

'Isaac'

Release: November 2005 **Album:** *Confessions on a Dance Floor*
Writers/Producers: Madonna, Stuart Price

The 'Isaac' in the title is the English translation of vocalist Yitzhak Sinwai's first name who reads excerpts of the Yemenite Hebrew poem 'Im Nin'alu'. 'Isaac' initially received criticism from Hebrew scholars as blasphemous, but Madonna pointed out the ancient words recited are 'if all of the doors of all of the generous peoples' homes are closed to you, the gates of heaven will always be open.' Sinwai, a study buddy of Madonna's, recorded his vocals for this transcendental dance track in a single take.

'Push'

Release: November 2005 **Album:** *Confessions on a Dance Floor*
Writers/Producers: Madonna, Stuart Price

The *Confessions* album's gushy valentine to husband Guy Ritchie, 'Push' might be the last true love song Madonna penned for him, if 2008's *Hard Candy* was their break-up album and 2012's *MDNA* the divorce aftermath. According to her brother, Christopher Ciccone, whose memoir *Life with My Sister Madonna* was published in 2008, Ritchie was homophobic, to which Ritchie pithily replied, 'you'd be hard pushed to be a homophobe and marry Madonna'. Maybe that was the 'push' Madonna was referring to! He and Madonna would divorce that same year.

'Like It or Not'

Release: November 2005 **Album:** *Confessions on a Dance Floor*
Writers: Madonna, Christian Karlsson, Pontus Winnberg, Henrik Jonback
Producers: Madonna, Bloodshy & Avant

Sinner and saint alike Madonna must have been partial enough to this song in its original version by Bloodshy & Avant not to insist Price mess with it in any way as *COADF* closer. Madonna gave a defiant performance of 'Like It or Not' on 2006's Confessions Tour ending with a backdrop projection of a rose blooming, while the likeable track popped up again during 2016's *Tears of a Clown* Miami show. Two electronica-infused 'Like It or Not' demos leaked in 2011.

'Fighting Spirit'

Release: November 2005 **Album:** *Confessions on a Dance Floor*
Writers/Producers: Madonna, Mirwais Ahmadzaï

A bonus track on the limited edition of *COADF*, this might just be the song where it became apparent Mirwais was not the man for the job of helping Madonna reclaim disco. In 2017, however, music blog MuuMuse took a different view insisting '"Fighting Spirit" is cool musically if only because it sounds like a demo that perfectly bridges the gap between the politically woke, introspective *American Life* and the escapist love letter to the dance floor that is *Confessions*'. Them's fighting words!

'Super Pop'

Release: November 2005 **Album:** *Confessions on a Dance Floor*
Writers/Producers: Madonna, Mirwais Ahmadzaï

A bonus track for members of Madonna's Icon fan club, on 'Super Pop' Madonna wants to be president—if she were a man. She also asserts she would be a lion, an Aston Martin, Isaac Newton, Martin Luther King, Marlon Brando, Frida Kahlo, a lemon drop, herself, Cassius Clay, intense, a dog, a man, and, yup, super pop. Oh, and different too, if she was president. A chugging demo of 'Super Pop' leaked in 2010 with a rockier edge amid insinuations it originally came from the 2000 *Music* sessions. In 2020, an earlier demo, 'Funny Game', leaked.

'History'

Year: 2006 **Single release:** October 2006 (B-side to 'Jump')
Writers/Producers: Madonna, Stuart Price

Ditched from *Confessions*, but manifesting as the B-side for 'Jump', 'History' is a welcome, if somewhat tame, plea for global reconciliation—'I have a dream but dreams are not for free/We all need to change or just repeat history'. Two unreleased demos, called 'History (Land of the Free)', leaked in 2007 and 2008 as earlier, audibly heavier, versions of 'History'. Amazingly, if not confoundingly, after the huge success of *Confessions*, Madonna and Price never recorded together again. As regards their personal history, Price became romantically involved with Angela Becker, Madonna's then co-manager. Becker left that role to have their first child, later becoming manager for Pet Shop Boys, for whom Price would produce numerous albums.

17

The *Hard Candy* Era

Hard Candy
Warner Bros. Records: 421372-2
Released: April 2008
Tracklist

'Candy Shop'	4:15
'4 Minutes'	4:04
'Give It 2 Me'	4:48
'Heartbeat'	4:04
'Miles Away'	4:49
'She's Not Me'	6:05
'Incredible'	6:20
'Beat Goes On'	4:27
'Dance 2Night'	5:03
'Spanish Lesson'	3:36
'Devil Wouldn't Recognize You'	5:09
'Voices'	3:39

Japanese, Spotify and iTunes Store pre-order bonus track

'Ring My Bell'	3:54

'Hey You'

Warner Bros. Records: 9362-49942-9 **MP3/WAV release:** May 2007
Compilation: *Live Earth: The Concerts for a Climate in Crisis*
Writer: Madonna
Producers: Madonna, Pharrell Williams

    Madonna's first self-penned song, and single, since 1985's 'Gambler' was all for a good cause, the *Live Earth* charity campaign. 'Hey You', featuring Mirwais on guitar, was released as a free download for a week—with Microsoft donating 25¢ per download to the Alliance for Global Climate Change cause—before becoming a regular digital single (and appearing on the *Live Earth* album). The song peaked at #187 in the UK, but due to it being a free download was ineligible for the US charts. Arriving more than a decade before Greta Thunberg galvanized the climate change movement, Madonna has only ever performed 'Hey You' the once at London's *Live Earth* concert in July 2007.

VID BIT!

Directors: Johan Söderberg & Marcus Lindkvist

Never officially released, but shown as the backdrop during Madonna's *Live Earth* rendition of 'Hey You', the video highlights her heroes John Lennon, Martin Luther King, Gandhi, Mother Teresa, Bob Dylan, Nelson Mandela, Aung San Suu Kyi, Al Gore, the Dalai Lama, and Albert Einstein.

'Sing' (Annie Lennox Featuring Various Artists)

Sony BMG: 88697284262 **Single release:** December 2007 **Album:** *Songs of Mass Destruction*
Writer: Annie Lennox
Producer: Glen Ballard

On 1 December, World AIDS Day, Annie Lennox released 'Sing' the second single from her *Songs of Mass Destruction* album. With its focus on empowering women around the world, especially HIV+ women, many female performers were keen to come on board to help sing the chorus when Lennox asked. Rather than merely joining the crowd Madonna sang the second verse of 'Sing', something Lennox was 'thrilled to bits' by. Their other twenty-three 'sisters' were Shakira, Pink, Céline Dion, k.d. lang, Isobel Campbell, Dido, Anastacia, Melissa Etheridge, Sugababes, KT Tunstall, Martha Wainwright, Gladys Knight, Beverley Knight, Bonnie Raitt, Sarah McLachlan, Angélique Kidjo, Faith Hill, Beth Gibbons, Fergie, Shingai Shoniwa, and Joss Stone. 'Sing' became a minor hit and snuck into the Top 20 of the US Dance Club Songs Chart. Lennox formed an NGO called SING, on the day *Sing* was released, to raise funds and awareness for HIV/AIDS. In October 2010 it was announced £100,000 had been raised.

VID BIT!

Editor: Scott Mele

Lennox, her South African activists and her empowering message of AIDS/HIV awareness are the stars here. Neither Madonna, nor any of the other female artists on 'Sing', appear.

Remix Fix!

British Indian artist Nitin Sawhney created an alternative version of 'Sing', while Dean Coleman, Harry 'Choo Choo' Romero, and Moto Blanco made the dance floor sing.

'4 Minutes'
(Featuring Justin Timberlake and Timbaland)

Warner Bros. Records: 9362-49868-2 **Single release:** March 2008 **Album:** *Hard Candy*
Writers: Madonna, Tim Mosley, Justin Timberlake, Nate Hills
Producers: Timbaland, Timberlake, Danja

'4 Minutes' was indeed the song that saved Madonna at US radio. The *Hard Candy* album's lead single, credited to Madonna featuring Justin Timberlake and Timbaland, peaked at #3 in the US. In twenty-one countries including the UK, Australia, Canada, Germany, and Netherlands '4 Minutes' raced to #1. Lyrically, '4 Minutes' was inspired by Madonna's visits to Malawi (documented in the film *I Am Because We Are* released the same year) about 'living on borrowed time'. *Hard Candy* debuted at #1 in thirty-seven countries and became 2008's eleventh biggest selling album, with Madonna's subsequent Sticky & Sweet Tour becoming the highest grossing tour by a solo artist in history, breaking a record Madonna had held with her previous Confessions Tour. '4 Minutes' received two Grammy nominations for Best Pop Collaboration with Vocals and Best Remixed Recording and was covered by the *Glee* TV series during *The Power of Madonna* episode in 2010, charting in the US Top 100.

Vid Bit!

Directors: Jonas & François

Featuring the choreography of Jamie King, '4 Minutes' was a futuristic, high concept effort, nominated for Best Dancing in a Video at the *MTV Video Music Awards* (losing to Pussycat Dolls' booby-trapped 'When I Grow Up').

Remix Fix!

A well-deserving Junkie XL was Grammy nominated for Best Remixed Recording for his efforts on '4 Minutes'.

'Candy Shop'

Release: April 2008 **Album:** *Hard Candy*
Writers: Madonna, Pharrell Williams
Producers: The Neptunes, Madonna

On *Hard Candy*, her final album with Warner Brothers and first in three years, Madonna chose to step away from dance music and instead towards her other love of urban and R&B grooves. Album opener 'Candy Shop' set the pace with an archetypal beat, courtesy of producers The Neptunes (Williams and Chad Hugo), ranked as that decade's #1 producers by *Billboard*. 'We were just in a studio,' Williams recalled about writing 'Candy Shop', 'and [Madonna] was like, "Look, give me some hot shit!"' 'Candy Shop', which chews on an elongated sex/candy metaphor, was the Sticky & Sweet Tour's opening number.

'Give It 2 Me'

Warner Bros. Records: 0-513014 **Single release:** June 2008 **Album:** *Hard Candy*
Writers: Madonna, Pharrell Williams
Producers: The Neptunes, Madonna

American radio's love affair with Madonna proved short-lived, especially minus the benefit of having Justin Timberlake attached. *Hard Candy*'s zingy second single, 'Give It 2 Me', written by Madonna as a ticking off to the music biz who thought her past her prime, appeared for one week only in the US Top 100 at a lowly #57, though it reached #7 in the UK and #1 in Hungary, Turkey, Spain and Netherlands. If it was any consolation 'Give It 2 Me' was nominated for a Grammy for Best Dance Recording. The closing number on the Sticky & Sweet Tour, during her MDNA Tour in 2012 in New York Madonna memorably performed 'Give It 2 Me' with Korean artist Psy, at the time the hottest new artist in the world due to his 'Gangnam Style' K-pop hit. 'Give It 2 Me' stands as the final Madonna single to be awarded a British sales accreditation (Silver) to date.

VID BIT!

Directors: Tom Munro and Nathan Rissman

Filmed during an *Elle* photoshoot a few months before her fiftieth birthday, 'Give It 2 Me' had Madonna back in a dance studio with Williams making a cameo. The interplay between him, Madonna and her handbag, is the video's true highlight.

REMIX FIX!

The Sly and Robbie Bongo Mix gave the song a different approach dousing it in a Jamaican dub feel, including a fierce rap from Cherine 'Dancehall Soul' Anderson.

'Heartbeat'

Release: April 2008 **Album:** *Hard Candy*
Writers: Madonna, Pharrell Williams
Producers: The Neptunes, Madonna

'Heartbeat' seemed like an obvious single choice, but *Hard Candy* only produced three hits—'4 Minutes', 'Give It 2 Me', and belatedly 'Miles Away'. Was 'Heartbeat' just the wrong song at the wrong time? With Madonna in the throes of her divorce from Guy Ritchie perhaps she just was not feeling it in her heartbeat anymore. A killer chorus, a deft groove from The Neptunes and Madonna both sexy and sweet at the same time, 'Heartbeat' was a readymade hit that never was. A demo version of the track, featuring Williams and Pussycat Dolls' lead singer Nicole Scherzinger, leaked in 2010.

'Miles Away'

Warner Bros. Records: 9362-49800-8 **Single release:** October 2008 **Album:** *Hard Candy*
Writers: Madonna, Tim Mosley, Justin Timberlake, Nate Hills
Producers: Timberland, Timberlake, Danja

Madonna's bittersweet last stand declaration to husband Guy Ritchie was *Hard Candy*'s third single, released in October 2008 at the same time as they reached a divorce settlement. Madonna sang 'Miles Away' on her Sticky & Sweet Tour after the split was announced and—gulp—dedicated the song to 'the emotionally retarded'. 'Miles Away' failed to find any radio support again in the US, missing the Top 100 completely. In the UK it scrapped into the Top 40 at #39, though reaching #1 in Spain. In Japan 'Miles Away' became a huge hit, used in a Japanese TV series called *Change*, as well as selling half a million ringtones, helping *Hard Candy* become one of Madonna's biggest selling albums in Japan in decades. From 'I Deserve It' to 'Love Profusion' to 'Push' to 'Miles Away', Ritchie was, if nothing more, a true blue muse to Madonna.

Vid Bit!
Director: Nathan Rissman

Madonna commissioned her former gardener, Rissman, also director of her 2008 *I Am Because We Are* doco, to create a virtual videologue from the Sticky & Sweet Tour.

Remix Fix!
Stuart Price served a pulsating Thin White Duke Remix owing a debt to the style of Peter Rauhofer, while Rebirth and Johnny Vicious took 'Miles Away' into

the big room club spaces. Morgan Page offered a phat bass remix, while Aaron LaCrate & Samir B-More brought 'Miles Away' to a technoclash zone.

'She's Not Me'

Release: April 2008 **Album:** *Hard Candy*
Writers: Madonna, Pharrell Williams
Producers: The Neptunes, Madonna

Gaga, ooh la la! Was the deeply dissing 'She's Not Me' directed at Lady Gaga, or some young pretender who had caught Guy Ritchie's eye? Performed on 2008–09's Sticky & Sweet Tour Madonna took the funky 'She's Not Me' and made it a true climax in front of a video of her own images and four iconic dancer 'replicas' of herself, telling the audience, 'Ladies, have you ever had a best friend who wanted to do everything you wanted to do, including fuck your boyfriend?' A typically melodramatic Offer Nissim remix, with a nod to ABBA's 1979 'Voulez-Vous' hit, leaked in 2009.

'Incredible'

Release: April 2008 **Album:** *Hard Candy*
Writers: Madonna, Pharrell Williams
Producers: The Neptunes, Madonna

If 'Miles Away' was Madonna's ode to the difficulty of her relationship with Guy Ritchie, long-distance or not, then 'Incredible' is her wishing she could go back to the moment when they first met and she felt something rather, well, incredible. Perhaps that thing Madonna missed most was their bedroom antics, as later on she coos 'sex with you is incredible'. While The Neptunes' production here traps the song very much in its era, the lyrics of 'Incredible' provide an indelible picture of Madonna's complicated life leading up to her divorce. Little wonder she posed as a boxer on the *Hard Candy* cover.

'Beat Goes On' (Featuring Kanye West)

Release: April 2008 **Album:** *Hard Candy*
Writers: Madonna, Pharrell Williams, Kanye West
Producers: The Neptunes, Madonna

While Timbaland and The Neptunes were already big names in the music biz at this stage, West was just on the cusp of superstardom. On the 'disco-hop' 'Beat Goes On', whose title references The Whispers 1980 disco hit 'And the Beat Goes On',

The Neptunes channel Chic in a tune not a million miles away from some of the material on Madonna's debut album. West's 'Beat Goes On' rap interlude includes the telling lines 'Fame is a drug wanna hit that?/'Cos I know exactly where to get that'. Madonna, a major fan, if not friend, dubbed Kanye 'the black Madonna'.

'Dance 2 Night'

Release: April 2008 **Album:** *Hard Candy*
Writers: Madonna, Tim Mosley, Justin Timberlake, Hannon Lane
Producers: Timberland, Justin Timberlake, Hannon Lane, Demacio 'Demo' Castellon
   'Dance 2 Night' is unquestionably the most 'disco' track on *Hard Candy* and perhaps the missing link between this and her previous *Confessions* album. Asked by MTV why she wanted to collaborate with well-known producers instead of unknowns like in the past, Madonna stated, 'because they're good, and I like their shit'. Never performed live, an unofficial hard house 'Dance 2 Night' remix by Peter Rauhofer appeared online two years before the Austrian DJ/remixer died in 2013.

'Spanish Lesson'

Release: April 2008 **Album:** *Hard Candy*
Writers: Madonna, Pharrell Williams
Producers: The Neptunes, Madonna
   With her last few albums missing out on their one Latin song quota, here Madonna reinstated that long-standing tradition. 'Spanish Lesson' was inspired by a high-energy Latin dance craze called The Percolator involving wildly gyrating your legs in time to the music as well as your booty. After performing it live on her Sticky & Sweet Tour with her dancers dressed as monks (and Madonna freestyling the percolator) 'Spanish Lesson' popped up again briefly during stops of 2012's MDNA Tour in Spanish-speaking countries. In its 2018 reassessment of *Hard Candy*, *Billboard* deemed the flamenco-flavoured 'Spanish Lesson' 'a guilty pleasure'.

'Devil Wouldn't Recognize You'

Release: April 2008 **Album:** *Hard Candy*
Writers: Madonna, Tim Mosley, Justin Timberlake, Nate Hills, Joe Henry
Producers: Timberland, Timberlake, Danja
   Timbaland's concept with his contributions to *Hard Candy* was to make something like 1983's 'Holiday' but with an R&B groove. The first track he

produced for the project was 'Devil Wouldn't Recognize You', which Madonna had been working on for some years previously. If the aim morphed to meld William Orbit's production with their own urban vibe, then they were devilishly close. Certainly, there is no misreading the lyrics here, which her brother-in-law, Henry, contributed to—Madonna was going through a messy, ugly, and sad divorce ('now that it's over you can lie to me right through your smile'). A demo of 'Devil Wouldn't Recognize You', with a lovely understated guitar solo, leaked some years later.

'Voices'

Release: April 2008 **Album:** *Hard Candy*
Writers: Madonna, Tim Mosley, Justin Timberlake, Nate Hills
Producers: Timbaland, Timberlake, Danja

Album closer 'Voices' continued the gloomy theme of a bad relationship ending badly from 'Devil Wouldn't Recognize You'. An orchestral version of *Voices* leaked a whole decade later providing a fresh take on one of Madonna's most underrated songs from one of her most underrated albums. On the tenth anniversary of its release in 2018, *Billboard* published a story headlined, 'Why *Hard Candy* is Madonna's Last Great Album' arguing it is 'from start to finish, the last great Madonna album, if not up to her outright classics'.

'Ring My Bell'

Release: April 2008 **Album:** *Hard Candy*
Writers: Madonna, Pharrell Williams
Producers: The Neptunes, Madonna

'If you want to talk to me that's exactly what you're going to have to do—talk to me,' Madonna proclaims at the beginning of this Japanese Spotify and iTunes pre-order bonus track from *Hard Candy*. 'Ring My Bell', which finds both Madonna and The Neptunes on mid-noughties autopilot, has her determined to withhold sex from a lover who can't say sorry, show any gratitude 'and once you attack you can't take it back' (now who could that be?). Williams also features briefly on backing vocals.

'Like an Angel Passing Through My Room'

Leak: August 16, 2008 (Madonna's fiftieth)
Writers: Benny Andersson, Björn Ulvaeus
Producers: Madonna, William Orbit

Never officially released, this soaring lullaby leaked, as if meant to be by the powers that be, on Madonna's fiftieth birthday, leading some to suggest it was fondly intended as a birthday present from the Queen of Pop to her fans. Not to be confused with her other two big 'like' hits, 'Like an Angel Passing Through My Room' is an ethereal cover of the song holding the dubious honour of being ABBA's last ever album track on 1981's *The Visitors* until their return *Voyage* forty years later in 2021.

'Get Stupid'

Warner Bros. Records: 521138-2 **Release:** March 2010 **Live album:** *Sticky & Sweet Tour*
Writer: Madonna
Producers: Johan Söderberg, Stuart Price

The sarcastic, if not sardonic, 'Get Stupid' very much follows on from Madonna's 2007 *Hey You* charity single. 'Get up/It's time/Your life/Your world' Madonna chants, borrowing lyrics from her Neptunes song 'Beat Goes On' from *Hard Candy* and fragments of beats from other *Hard Candy* tracks. Regular Madonna video collaborator Söderberg remixed and directed the two 'Get Stupid' backdrop projections, curated by photographer Steven Klein, which appeared during Madonna's Sticky & Sweet Tour.

18

The *Celebration* Era

Celebration
Warner Bros. Records: 521096-2
Released: September 2009
Tracklist
Disc One

'Hung Up'	5:38
'Music'	3:45
'Vogue'	5:16
'4 Minutes'	3:09
'Holiday'	6:08
'Everybody'	4:10
'Like a Virgin'	3:09
'Into the Groove'	4:45
'Like a Prayer'	5:42
'Ray of Light'	4:33
'Sorry'	3:58
'Express Yourself'	4:00
'Open Your Heart'	3:49
'Borderline'	3:59
'Secret'	4:28
'Erotica'	4:30
'Justify My Love'	4:54
'Revolver'	3:40

Disc Two

'Dress You Up'	4:02
'Material Girl'	4:00
'La Isla Bonita'	4:04
'Papa Don't Preach'	4:29

'Lucky Star'	3:38
'Burning Up'	3:44
'Crazy for You'	3:44
'Who's That Girl'	4:00
'Frozen'	6:18
'Miles Away'	3:45
'Take a Bow'	5:20
'Live to Tell'	5:51
'Beautiful Stranger'	4:22
'Hollywood'	4:23
'Die Another Day'	4:36
'Don't Tell Me'	4:11
'Cherish'	3:51
'Celebration'	3:34
Digital Deluxe Edition	
'Celebration' (Benny Benassi Remix Edit)	3:58
Amazon MP3 deluxe edition	
'It's So Cool'	3:27

(Also released as single disc eighteen-track collection with the same title on Warner Bros. Records 9362499274)

'Celebration'

Warner Bros. Records: 9362-49714-8 **Single release:** July 2009 **Compilation:** *Celebration*
Writers: Madonna, Paul Oakenfold, Ian Green, Ciaran Gribbin
Producers: Madonna, Paul Oakenfold, Ian Green

'Celebration' was one of two new tracks on the *Celebration* best of, available as a standard eighteen-track set, or deluxe edition with thirty-six tracks. The first single from Madonna's fourth hits compilation heralded a welcome return to the dance floor after 2008's *Hard Candy*. 'Celebration' managed to spend one week in the US Top 100 at #71, yet hit #3 in the UK. The infinitely superior Benny Benassi remix was used for the music video, while 'Celebration' received a Grammy nomination for Best Dance Recording.

VID BIT!
Director: Jonas Åkerlund

Filmed in Milan/Barcelona during the Sticky & Sweet Tour, with fans invited to take part, also appearing were Madonna's then boyfriend, model/DJ Jesus Luz, and daughter Lourdes. An alternate cut, aka the 'fan version', was released on Madonna's MySpace page with extra footage and cameos by Oakenfold and Åkerlund.

Remix Fix!

The Benny Benassi Remix (by Benny and cousin Alle) grabbed a somewhat standard trance-pop record, transforming it into one of the best remixes of Madonna's career. Thanks to their work here the Benassi pair were smartly enlisted for her next album.

'Revolver' (Featuring Lil Wayne)

Warner Bros. Records: 9362-49685-8 **Single release:** December 2009
Compilation: *Celebration*
Writers: Madonna, Dwayne Carter, Justin Franks, Carlos Centel Battey, Steven Andre Battey, Brandon Kitchen
Producers: Madonna, Frank E

Keeping one foot on the dance floor, but the other very much in the urban club next door, the second new *Celebration* track, 'Revolver', originally called 'Die Happy', was released three months after the album just before Christmas, alas minus video. Featuring a rap by Lil Wayne, Madonna's 'sex pistol' unhappily misfired on both the UK and US charts and was nowhere to be seen. Producer Frank E later complained Warner Bros used a rough mix of 'Revolver' with the vocals too low, refusing to let him fix it. A demo of 'Revolver', by R&B singer/songwriter RaVaughn, leaked some months prior to the release of the *Celebration* compilation. Was Madonna so intent on releasing this track ('I had a bullet with you name on it') because *Revolver* was also the title of her ex-husband's 2005 movie? A battered Madonna had just fired the first missive in an ugly battle that would culminate three years later in *MDNA*'s violently unhappy 'Gang Bang'.

Vid Bit!

None—what were they thinking! Someone should be shot!

Remix Fix!

Although 'Revolver' peaked at #4 on the US Dance Club Songs chart, its David Guetta and Afrojack One Love remix won a Grammy for Best Remixed Recording in 2011.

'It's So Cool'

Release: September 2009 **Compilation:** *Celebration*
Writers: Madonna, Mirwais Ahmadzaï, Monte Pittman
Producers: Madonna, Paul Oakenfold

Written for the discarded Luc Besson movie project and intended to be a folk tune in the style of The Kinks, Madonna reworked 'It's So Cool' with Paul Oakenfold as an iTunes bonus track on her *Celebration* greatest hits collection. Mirwais later called it 'a failure' adding he 'approved it, but I didn't think it would end up being such a mess'. The original 2002 Mirwais demos emerged a year after the Oakenfold version. Sporting a much less polished edge, the ironic lyrics made much more sense, with the added benefit of Madonna minus any vocal retuning.

'Broken (I'm Sorry)'

7″ release (Icon Fan Club only): October 2012
Writers: Madonna, Paul Oakenfold, Ian Green, Ciaran Gribbin
Producers: Madonna, Paul Oakenfold

'Sorry Part II'? With Madonna chanting 'don't you feel sorry', here's another tried-out then left off track from the *Celebration* album and another sorry-not-sorry sore kiss-off to by now ex-husband Guy Ritchie ('A lesson that I needed to learn/But that doesn't mean that it doesn't burn'). An early acoustic demo version of 'Broken (I'm Sorry)' leaked online in 2011, but the finished version got an official release in 2012 as a promotional vinyl single for Icon fan club members. The seven-minute Original Extended Mix leaked in 2012 proving' Broken (I'm Sorry)' might have been a better *Celebration* second single choice than 'Revolver'.

19

The *MDNA* Era

MDNA
Interscope Records: 0602527977515
Released: March 2012
Standard Edition Tracklist

'Girl Gone Wild'	3:43
'Gang Bang'	5:26
'I'm Addicted'	4:33
'Turn Up the Radio'	3:46
'Give Me All Your Luvin''	3:22
'Some Girls'	3:53
'Superstar'	3:55
'I Don't Give A'	4:19
'I'm a Sinner'	4:52
'Love Spent'	3:46
'Masterpiece'	3:59
'Falling Free'	5:13

Deluxe Edition bonus tracks

'Beautiful Killer'	3:49
'I Fucked Up'	3:29
'B-Day Song'	3:33
'Best Friend'	3:20

'Give Me All Your Luvin''
(Featuring Nicki Minaj & M.I.A.)

Interscope Records: 0602527974569 **Single release:** February 2012 **Album:**
MDNA

Writers: Madonna, Martin Solveig, Onika Tanya Maraj, Maya Arulpragasam, Michael Tordjman
Producers: Madonna, Martin Solveig

The first of her three albums for new label Interscope, via her 360 deal with Live Nation, *MDNA* was buoyed by the then soaring EDM (electronic dance music) movement, of which her music had been a truly pioneering force. The first single, 'Give Me All Your Luvin'', featuring guest spots from rapper Nicki Minaj and artist/activist M.I.A., leaked in November 2011, three months ahead of its scheduled release. A Spanish Madonna fan was subsequently arrested and charged. The bubble-gum pop 'GMAYL' with its cheerleading refrain was properly debuted at the Super Bowl XLVI halftime show in February 2012, becoming Madonna's thirty-eighth US Top 10 hit, peaking at #10, though it reached a worrisome #37 in the UK. 'GMAYL' was performed during 2012's MDNA Tour as a cheerleading extravaganza, no doubt reminding Madonna of her own high school days as a cheerleader.

VID BIT!

Director: Megaforce

The 'GMAYL' video kicks off with a perplexing axiom ('Fans can make you famous, a contract can make you rich, the press can make you a superstar, but only luv can make you a player') flashed against a brick wall before M.I.A. and Minaj bust Madonna out of her house pushing a baby pram. Once that was handed over, she struts past American football players removing her coat to reveal the sexy Madonna of old in a timely Super Bowl tie-in. Touchdown!

REMIX FIX!

Having just performed at the *Super Bowl* with LMFAO, they dispensed a sexy/speedy Party Rock Remix before going on indefinite hiatus.

'Girl Gone Wild'

Interscope Records: 0602537015177 **Single release:** March 2012 **Album:** *MDNA*
Writers: Madonna, Jenson Vaughan, Alle Benassi, Benny Benassi
Producers: Madonna, Benny Benassi, Alle Benassi

'Girl Gone Wild' was not just the *MDNA* opener and subsequent MDNA Tour partystarter, but clearly Madonna's state of mind as an unrepentant single lady ready to indulge life's pleasures again. 'Girl Gone Wild' was like 'Into the Groove' on meth not MDMA—a mad techno rush of unrelenting gay abandon. Despite the references to her own musical past, Cyndi Lauper's 1983 'Girls Just Want to Have Fun' hit and some liquor product placement, 'Girl Gone Wild' missed the US Top 100. In the UK it peaked at #73 and in Australia at #93, though it went platinum in the Benassis' home country of Italy. In 2012 Canadian artist Rosette Luve posted a version of 'Girl Gone Wild' online claiming she had co-written the song.

VID BIT!

Directors: Mert and Marcus

Photographers Mert and Marcus, who also shot the album covers for *MDNA*, were brought on board to direct 'Girl Gone Wild'. It was literally a monochromatic Madonna photoshoot gone wild, complete with hunky male models and Ukrainian group Kazaky sashaying in formation in heels.

REMIX FIX!

Israeli DJ diva Offer Nissim, Madonna's remixer of choice for most of the next decade, made his first appearance here as an official remixer. The other important remix was Avicii's UMF Mix, which he debuted with Madonna/'Molly' at Miami's Ultra Music Festival.

'Gang Bang'

Release: March 2012 **Album:** *MDNA*
Writers: Madonna, William Orbit, Priscilla Hamilton, Keith Harris, Jean-Baptiste, Mika, Don Juan Demacio 'Demo' Casanova, Stephen Kozmeniuk
Producers: Madonna, William Orbit, The Demolition Crew

If anything, 'Gang Bang' is a true companion piece to 1992's vitriolic 'Thief of Hearts'. British pop star Mika was involved in the song's writing, noting it was called 'Gang Bang', 'probably because there were so many people who worked on it'. Was the reason 'Gang Bang' is so angry because Madonna's ex-husband Guy Ritchie had fathered another son? *Rolling Stone* called *MDNA* 'a disco-fied divorce record' while *Glamour* magazine called it the 'ultimate divorce album'. Returning producer Orbit conceded it was aggressive and 'dark'. 'Gang Bang' was performed on 2012's MDNA Tour in a style befitting a Tarantino movie, complete with hard liquor, seedy motel and gun violence. An early demo of 'Gang Bang' leaked in 2012 sung by co-writer Hamilton (known by her stage name Priscilla Renea).

'I'm Addicted'

Release: March 2012 **Album:** *MDNA*
Writers: Madonna, Alle Benassi, Benny Benassi
Producers: Madonna, Alle Benassi, Benny Benassi, The Demolition Crew

The Benassi boys were back again for another crack with their then very of-the-minute Euro-techno beats and Madonna's drug-dipped lyrics. The middle eight of the song bears some similarity to Chris Brown's addictive 'Beautiful People' track the Benassis produced the previous year, which wound up a breakout EDM track. A high-energy, if not heavy-metal inspired, performance on 2012's MDNA Tour injected 'I'm Addicted' to another level.

'Turn Up the Radio'

Interscope Records: 06225276443282 **Single release:** June 2012
Album: MDNA
Writers: Madonna, Martin Solveig, Michael Tordjman, Jade Williams
Producers: Madonna, Martin Solveig

The final *MDNA* single was also the first song for the entire *MDNA* project Madonna said yes to. Co-writer Williams was also known professionally as Sunday Girl/Whinnie Williams, with 'Turn Up the Radio' originally slated for Solveig's *Smash* album. The poppy 'Turn Up the Radio' missed the UK and US Top 100, though it became a minor hit in Belgium, Spain, and Japan. Turned into a lively crowd singalong (with Madonna on guitar) during 2012's MDNA Tour, the original 'Turn Up the Radio', by Martin Solveig featuring Sunday Girl, leaked online in 2017 with significantly different lyrics.

Vid Bit!
Director: Tom Munro

Madonna driving around Florence, Italy, picking up handsome men (including then boyfriend and *MDNA* backing dancer Brahim Zaibat) and having fun—all in a day's work, especially if you have a music video to film while on tour! 'Turn Up the Radio' is one of the most giddishly goofy videos Madonna has ever produced.

Remix Fix!
Offer Nissim, R3hab and the song's producer himself, Martin Solveig, all dusted, polished and turned up this maddening-crowd pleaser, while the Laidback Luke Alternative Remix featured a raucous rap by Far East Movement.

'Some Girls'

Release: March 2012 **Album:** *MDNA*
Writers/Producers: Madonna, William Orbit, Klas Åhlund

Inspired by the Dutch 'hardstyle' electronic dance genre, mixing techno and hardcore with distorted synths and discordant sounds, this was not Orbit's finest work. Madonna goes heavy on the Auto-Tune, dissing all those other girls 'who are not like me', though the self-referential nod to *Like a Virgin* is endearing.

Madonna presumably was not so fussed on 'Some Girls' as it did not make the set list for 2012's MDNA Tour. A demo purporting to be the original version leaked online in 2014. Running at over nine minutes it turns 'Some Girls' into a major epic that in its album form peaked too soon.

'Superstar'

Release: March 2012 **Album:** *MDNA*
Writers/Producers: Madonna, Hardy 'Indigo' Muanza, Michael Malih

Madonna flicks through her encyclopedia to compare her own 'superstar' with eight other historical figures—actor Marlon Brando, basketball great Michael Jordan, gangster Al Capone, Roman emperor Caesar, American president Abraham Lincoln, martial arts movie star Bruce Lee, movie star John Travolta, and film legend James Dean. Only released in Brazil as a promotional single, 'Superstar' came in its original album form with the bonus of a club-ready Eddie Amador dance remix. 'Superstar' also featured mini-superstar backing vocals from daughter Lourdes, credited as Lola Leon. Tabloid reports insisted Madonna planned to make a video for 'Superstar' dressed as a 'Terror Bride' (a combination of a traditional Iraqi bridal veil and a US soldier's uniform), but, if so, sensibly accepted the advice not to go there.

'I Don't Give A' (Featuring Nicki Minaj)

Release: March 2012 **Album:** *MDNA*
Writers: Madonna, Martin Solveig, Onika Tanya Maraj, Julien Jabre
Producers: Madonna, Martin Solveig

The strident 'I Don't Give A' (you can guess the rest) was another angry rebuttal to the world—'Wake up ex-wife/This is your life/Children on your own/Turning on the telephone'. All this was before she really got stuck into ex-husband Guy Ritchie too. 'You were so mad at me/Who's got custody/ Lawyers suck it up/Didn't have a pre-nup' does not just hint, but screams, at what was going on in Madonna's life. Played live on 2012's MDNA Tour, 'I Don't Give A' was true detachment therapy.

'I'm a Sinner'

Release: March 2012 **Album:** *MDNA*
Writers: Madonna, William Orbit, Jean-Baptiste Kouame
Producers: Madonna, William Orbit

Picking up where 1998's 'Shanti/Ashtangi' dropped out, 'I'm a Sinner' is Madonna and Orbit once again on an eastern experience (there is that 'Beautiful Stranger' beat again). In 2014, Orbit gave his harsh appraisal of *MDNA* stating he would have 'dropped three of the six tracks produced by the other guys, they were not good enough in my opinion; too puerile. As for the remaining three I would have suggested to put more depth and make them more special.' Orbit added that if he had executive produced *MDNA* he 'could have done an absolutely exceptional job, something as powerful as *Ray of Light*'.

Love Spent

Release: March 2012 **Album:** *MDNA*
Writers: Madonna, William Orbit, Jean-Baptiste, Priscilla Hamilton, Alain Whyte, Ryan Buendia, Michael McHenry
Producers: Madonna, William Orbit, Free School

MDNA marked not only the first of Madonna's three albums with Interscope, but the first with Guy Oseary as her sole manager. *MDNA* went to #1 in the UK, US, Australia, Canada, Brazil, Mexico, and most of Europe and was Russia's top selling album of 2012. Tracks such as the gorgeous 'Falling Free' and post-Guy Ritchie divorce kiss-off 'Love Spent' might have sat comfortably on a natural successor to *Ray of Light*. 'Love Spent' may be the true heir to 1989's divorce pay-up ditty 'Till Death Do Us Part', with an exquisite acoustic version included on the Deluxe iTunes edition.

'Masterpiece'

Interscope Records: 0602527947310 **Single release:** March 2012 **Album:** *MDNA* **Soundtrack:** *W.E. (Music From The Motion Picture)*
Writers: Madonna, Julie Frost, Jimmy Harry
Producers: Madonna, William Orbit, Jimmy Harry

Written almost as an afterthought for her major movie directorial debut, *W.E.*, 'Masterpiece' was *MDNA*'s unofficial/promo single. Madonna was inspired to write it after constantly staring at her *W.E.* co-star Andrea Riseborough's face during filming. Asked if this was true by your author some years later, Riseborough replied with a laugh, 'it's very sweet to believe that'. The movie itself earned long-time Madonna stalwart Arianna Phillips an Oscar nomination for Best Costume Design, while 'Masterpiece' won Best Original Song at the Golden Globes, much to fellow nominee Elton John's chagrin. 'Masterpiece' peaked at #68 in the UK, but topped the charts in Russia.

Remix Fix!
A more radio-friendly Kid Capri remix of 'Masterpiece' appeared on the
Nightlife Edition remix EP of *MDNA*.

'Falling Free'

Release: March 2012 **Album:** *MDNA*
Writers: Madonna, Laurie Mayer, William Orbit, Joe Henry
Producers: Madonna, William Orbit

The final track on the standard *MDNA* (and Madonna's favourite of her Orbit
collabs) is a gorgeous ballad highlight, with Henry's added twisted lyrical flair.
With fans and critics alike questioning the singles choices, Orbit weighed into the
fracas. On Facebook he ranted about how the producers were 'pushed for time'
due to Madonna's business schedule. He claimed the album's failure was due
to 'various pressing commitments that took up the artist's limited time, such as
perfume ranges and teen fashion contests and other such endeavours which are
beyond my own limited understanding of pop star agendas'. A month later Orbit
apologised for his outburst stating: 'The *MDNA* comments. I should not have
said them publicly.' Orbit and Madonna would never work together again and, to
quote 'Falling Free', he was 'free to go'. In 2021, he called the response to *MDNA*
'disappointing', adding ageism had 'a profound negative effect' on its reception.

'Beautiful Killer'

Release: March 2012 **Album:** *MDNA*
Writers: Madonna, Martin Solveig, Michael Tordjman
Producers: Madonna, Martin Solveig

The first of four bonus tracks on the *MDNA* deluxe edition, 'Beautiful Killer' was
inspired by classic 1976 French crime noir movie *Le Samouraï* starring Alain Delon.
This killer overlooked track alludes to Delon's hitman character in *Le Samouraï*,
but the line 'can't really talk with a gun in my mouth', is Madonna again shooting
for her handsome ex. 'You're a beautiful killer, but you'll never be Alain Delon,' she
spits out at the end before a gunshot rings out. Ooh, that hurts.

'I Fucked Up'

Release: March 2012 **Album:** *MDNA*
Writers: Madonna, Martin Solveig, Julien Jabre
Producers: Madonna, Martin Solveig

'I fucked up/I made a mistake' is Madonna mourning the loss of her marriage, but now putting the onus on herself as 'nobody does it better than myself'. 'I blamed you when things didn't go my way,' she bays almost as if trying to repair the damage a little too late, chaffing about how she should have done what she was told and 'in front of you I was cold'. By comparison to 'Gang Bang', here Madonna is contrite, apologetic, and remorseful, with 'I Fucked Up' another underrated track from an album that often howls like a *Nasty Divorces for Dummies* audiobook.

'B-Day Song' (Featuring M.I.A.)

Release: March 2012 **Album:** *MDNA*
Writers: Madonna, Maya Arulpragasam, Martin Solveig
Producers: Madonna, Martin Solveig

'B-Day Song' marks the second appearance of M.I.A. (Arulpragasam). Like a bratty kid sister to 'Beautiful Stranger', Solveig apes Orbit's swinging '60s vibe with a tune plundered from Madonna's punk past. 'B-Day Song' at least lightens the mood of *MDNA* with some welcome relief from all of the post-marriage interrogation, though in 2016 M.I.A. accused Madonna, as well as Beyoncé and Rihanna, of stealing her sound. In 2020 *Glamour* magazine ruthlessly ranked 'B-Day Song' as the worst Madonna song of all time calling it 'truly unsalvageable'.

'Best Friend'

Release: March 2012 **Album:** *MDNA*
Writers: Madonna, Alle Benassi, Benny Benassi
Producers: Madonna, Alle Benassi, Benny Benassi, The Demolition Crew

As Madonna reflects on her marriage breakdown ('an intellectual with talent, what a catch'), sonically 'Best Friend' is a brave if hastily passé experiment in pushing the boundaries of what the Benassis did. 'Best Friend' was used as an MDNA Tour backdrop/dance interlude, mixed together with *Hard Candy*'s 'Heartbreak', amid scenes of a graveyard, funeral and angels to emphasis the death of a relationship. With the words 'it's so sad that it had to end' Madonna's second divorce album was done.

20

The *Rebel Heart* Era

Rebel Heart
Interscope Records/Live Nation: B0022740-02
Released: March 2015
Standard Edition Tracklist
'Living for Love'	3:38
'Devil Pray'	4:05
'Ghosttown'	4:09
'Unapologetic Bitch'	3:51
'Illuminati'	3:44
'Bitch I'm Madonna'	3:47
'Hold Tight'	3:37
'Joan of Arc'	4:01
'Iconic'	4:33
'HeartBreakCity'	3:33
'Body Shop'	3:39
'Holy Water'	4:09
'Inside Out'	4:23
'Wash All Over Me'	4:00

Deluxe Edition bonus tracks
'Best Night'	3:33
'Veni Vidi Vici'	4:39
'S.E.X.'	4:11
'Messiah'	3:22
'Rebel Heart'	3:21

Super Deluxe Edition bonus tracks
'Beautiful Scars'	4:19
'Borrowed Time'	3:24
'Addicted'	3:33

'Graffiti Heart'   3:39
Media Markt bonus track (Germany)
'Auto-Tune Baby'   4:00

'Living for Love'

Interscope Records/Live Nation: 0602547226396 **Single release:** December
2014 **Album:** *Rebel Heart*
Writers: Madonna, Diplo, Maureen McDonald, Toby Gad, Ariel Rechtshaid
Producers: Madonna, Diplo, Ariel Rechtshaid

The first single from *Rebel Heart*, Madonna's thirteenth studio album, found her
in a more hopeful post-breakup mood than on *MDNA* ('I found freedom in the ugly
truth/I deserve the best and it's not you'). Featuring Alicia Keys on piano (she also
added keys on 'Messiah' and 'Devil Pray'), the launch of self-love empowerment
mantra 'Living for Love' will perhaps always regrettable be linked to Madonna
toppling over during her performance of it at the BRIT Awards. Voted 'Most
shocking Celebrity Moment of 2015' by the UK's Channel 5, 'Living for Love' still
became Madonna's seventy-first Top 40 British hit (despite an ageist radio boycott),
though it went Top 10 in Israel, Finland, and Sweden. A year later, Madonna called
her on-stage slip-up 'the most embarrassing moment of my life'.

Vɪᴅ Bɪᴛ!
Director: J.A.C.K.

French duo Julien Choquart and Camille Hirigoyen (aka J.A.C.K.) decided
that rather than Madonna watching a matador she would become the matador.
Despite Madonna's avowed intention to 'bring a painting to life', the 'Living for
Love' video was superseded by her BRIT slip.

Rᴇᴍɪx Fɪx!
Offer Nissim brought the drama to the dancefloor (and the 'Living for Love' CD
single B-side).

'Devil Pray'

Release: December 2014 **Album:** *Rebel Heart*
Writers: Madonna, Avicii, Arash Pournouri, Carl Falk, Rami Yacoub, Savan
Kotecha, Dacoury Natche, Michael Tucker
Producers: Madonna, Avicii, DJ Dahl, Michael Diamonds

While the *Rebel Heart* album was officially set for release in March 2015, six
tracks were pre-released due to leaks just before Christmas 2014 (see Chapter

21). Many of those leaked demos (including a much poppier 'Devil Pray') were songs produced by Avicii, leading journalist/critic Roger Friedman to state, 'Madonna's leaked album may be her best'. The healing power of cleansing water once again returns here as a metaphor for keeping Madonna safe from a litany of evils amid a plush, languid beat.

'Ghosttown'

Interscope Records/Live Nation: 0602547344540 **Single release:** March 2015
Album: *Rebel Heart*
Writers: Madonna, Jason Evigan, Sean Douglas, Evan Bogart
Producers: Madonna, Jason Evigan, Billboard

The sad truth is if 'Ghosttown' had been released by Madonna during her first two decades of stardom it would have been a megahit. Instead, as *Rebel Heart*'s elegiac second single, 'Ghosttown' went ignored, or worse, unheard. Diplo would later complain 'Ghosttown' was 'a guaranteed Number One for anybody else, but she didn't get a fair shot'. 'Ghosttown' did become a US #1 on the Dance Club Charts, but in the UK peaked at #117 and did not enter the US, or Australian, Top 100. *Rolling Stone* ranked 'Ghosttown' #16 on its list of fifty best songs of 2015. Notably it was also the last Madonna song to get a CD single release.

Vid Bit!

Director: Jonas Åkerlund

Madonna in a scorched Agent Provocateur bra foresees the apocalypse with co-star/dance partner Terrence Howard, whose *Empire* TV series soundtrack kept *Rebel Heart* from debuting at #1 in the US. *Slant* magazine deemed the 'Ghosttown' video 'ruin porn'.

Remix Fix!

Armand Van Helden gave his 'Ghosttown' a polished dub makeover, Redtop's 'If I Were a Carpenter Remix' channelled James Bond, Austin Powers, and Nouvelle Vague, while Don Diablo made it into a techno-pop stormer.

'Unapologetic Bitch'

Release: December 2014 **Album:** *Rebel Heart*
Writers: Madonna, Diplo, Shelco Garcia, Bryan Orellana, Maureen McDonald, Toby Gad
Producers: Madonna, Shelco Garcia & Teenwolf, BV, Diplo, Ariel Rechtshaid

'Unapologetic Bitch' was also an early title for the *Rebel Heart* album. The first of *Rebel Heart*'s two 'bitch' songs, 'Unapologetic Bitch' was performed gleefully on the Rebel Heart Tour with a different special guest every night (Ariana Grande, Amy Schumer, and Katy Perry were just three of Madonna's support bitches). Madonna returned the favour to Grande by providing the voice of 'God' in her 2018 'God is a Woman' video. 'Unapologetic Bitch', like 'Living for Love', appears lyrically to be inspired by Madonna's three-year romance with choreographer/dancer Brahim Zaibat. Ahead of the release of 'Unapologetic Bitch', British tabloids bitchily declared, 'Madonna lashes out at toyboy ex Brahim Zaibat's sexual prowess and lack of wealth'.

'Illuminati'

Release: December 2014 **Album:** *Rebel Heart*
Writers: Madonna, Maureen McDonald, Toby Gad, Larry Griffin Jr, Mike Dean, Kanye West, Ernest Brown, Jacques Webster
Producers: Madonna, Kanye West, Mike Dean, Symbolyc One, Charlie Heat, Travis Scott

Another of the six tracks rushed released in December 2014 to get ahead of the *Rebel Heart* leaks, on 'Illuminati' Madonna name names of 'everybody in this party shining like illuminati'—Jay-Z, Beyoncé, Nicki Minaj, Lil Wayne, Oprah, Obama, The Pope, Rihanna, Queen Elizabeth, Kanye West, Lady Gaga, Steve Jobs, Bill Gates, Justin Bieber, LeBron James, and Hilary Clinton. Luxury brands Gucci and Prada also get a namecheck, as do ISIS and Google. Co-produced by West, who that same year married Kim Kardashian, Madonna wrote trend-conscious 'Illuminati' after she was accused of being part of 'a group of powerful, successful people who are working behind the scenes to control the universe'.

'Bitch I'm Madonna' (Featuring Nicki Minaj)

Interscope Records/Live Nation: Digital only **Single release:** June 2015 **Album:** *Rebel Heart*
Writers: Madonna, Diplo, Ariel Rechtshaid, Maureen McDonald, Toby Gad, Onika Maraj, Samuel Long
Producers: Madonna, Diplo

The third single from *Rebel Heart* was Madonna refusing to be 'age appropriate', like a bad frat girl on a bridal party weekend ready to 'go hard or go home all night long'. Minaj rapped 'Bitch I'm Madonna these hoes know', which might be the most nonsensical declaration to ever appear in a Madonna song. One of the six tracks rush-released for *Rebel Heart*, this impaired its later chart performance as a single, yet it became the only *Rebel Heart* track to break into the US Top 100 (at #84, thanks to video play finally being included). At its time of release, Madonna told *US Weekly* 'Bitch I'm Madonna' is her own all-time favourite song. Scottish co-writer Long, who later came out as trans artist Sophie, called their one-off track 'a happy coincidence. I felt a connection with the title'. Tragically Sophie slipped to their death in 2021 aged thirty-four.

Vid Bit!

Director: Jonas Åkerlund

Taking a leaf out of her one-shot performance of it on *The Tonight Show Starring Jimmy Fallon,* Åkerlund's video for 'Bitch I'm Madonna' featured cameos from Madonna's sons David and Rocco, Miley Cyrus, Katy Perry, Kanye West, Chris Rock, Jeremy Scott, Rita Ora, Jon Kortajarena, Alexander Wang, Arianne Phillips, and Beyoncé, while Nicki Minaj phoned in her pink-haired rap. The age-inappropriate 'Bitch I'm Madonna' video was proof you can still be a bad bitch post menopause.

Remix Fix!

Sander Kleinenberg achieved the no mean feat of retaining the original's flavour, but recreating it as a dancefloor bomb. A remix video of Madonna dancing to his 'bitch' in one of her own Rebel Heart Tour T-shirts was later recut.

'Hold Tight'

Universal: 3655278 2626 **Single release:** July 2015 (Italy) **Album:** *Rebel Heart*
Writers: Madonna, Diplo, Maureen McDonald, Toby Gad, Uzoechi Emenikie, Philip Meckseper
Producer: Madonna

Very much a classic era Madonna mid-tempo ballad, giving a very knowing nod at William Orbit's *Ray of Light* vintage, the song's co-writer Emenikie is better known by his performer name of MNEK. 'Hold Tight' became the third single from *Rebel Heart* in Italy, sent to radio there in July 2015, after it was released globally in February as part of the official release of the *Rebel Heart* album via the 'instant grat' for pre-ordering the album. A slew of demo versions leaked, ranging from more EDM-based to funk-pop, hinting at how Madonna struggled with 'Hold Tight'. Unusually, Madonna got a sole producer credit (her first) on the *Rebel Heart* version.

'Joan of Arc'

Release: March 2015 **Album:** *Rebel Heart*
Writers: Madonna, Toby Gad, Maureen McDonald, Larry Griffin Jr
Producers: Madonna, Toby Gad, AFSHeen, Josh Cumbee

Was there ever a better two-liner summary of Madonna's lifegoal than 'I'm not Joan of Arc/Not yet'? Acoustic Madonna makes her delayed, albeit welcome, return on 'Joan of Arc', released together with 'Ironic' and 'Hold Tight' as the second bundle of tracks from *Rebel Heart*. Madonna also posed as Joan of Arc on the inside sleeve of *Rebel Heart*. Leaked versions of 'Joan of Arc' included an all-acoustic folk version, virtually the same version Madonna performed live on *Ellen* in 2015. Madonna debuted 'Joan of Arc' during her Melbourne *Tears of a Clown* gig.

'Iconic'
(Featuring Chance The Rapper & Mike Tyson)

Release: March 2015 **Album:** *Rebel Heart*
Writers: Madonna, Toby Gad, Maureen McDonald, Larry Griffin Jr, Chancelor Bennett, Dacoury Natche, Michael Tucker
Producers: Madonna, Toby Gad, AFSHeen, Cumbee, DJ Dahi, Michael Diamonds

Boxer Mike Tyson opens 'Iconic' bragging, 'I'm the best the world has ever seen/I'm somebody you'll never forget 'cos I work hard and sweat in my tears/ I'm never falling again and if I did I'd come back'. Tyson later revealed he adlibbed the speech on the spot in one take in the studio. 'Iconic' also featured Chance The Rapper, who the following year won a Grammy for Best Rap Album. His rap is most interesting for the line 'Madonna said I remind her of Michael' (Jackson?). 'Iconic' had its big moment, however, as the opening number on her Rebel Heart Tour.

'HeartBreakCity'

Release: March 2015 **Album:** *Rebel Heart*
Writers: Madonna, Avicii, Arash Pournouri, Tobias Jimson, Michel Flygare, Paloma Stoecker, Salem Al Fakir, Magnus Lidehall, Vincent Pontare
Producers: Madonna, Avicii, Salem Al Fakir, Magnus Lidehall, Vicent Pontare, Astma & Rocwell

With various demos of 'HeartBreakCity' ranging from piano ballad to dance imprints, and then a much darker industrial ballad, once again it seemed as if

Madonna could not decide whether to go pop, or dance, but thankfully the finished version omitted its ungainly 'and I still feel shitty' lyric. A bruised, battered and 'fucked up' Madonna brutally takes her ex to task here. With lyrics lashing out again at a no-good lover ('Cut me down the middle/Fucked me up a little') was 'HeartBreakCity' directed at Brahim Zaibat, or stretching further back to Guy Ritchie? To overemphasis the love sick point, when Madonna sang 'HeartBreakCity' live on her Rebel Heart Tour it segued into 'Love Don't Live Here Anymore'.

'Body Shop'

Release: March 2015 **Album:** *Rebel Heart*
Writers: Madonna, Toby Gad, Maureen McDonald, Larry Griffin Jr, Dacoury Natche, Michael Tucker
Producers: Madonna, DJ Dahi, Michael Diamonds, Toby Gad

A song built around puns to do with getting serviced like a car ('I need a tune up') 'Body Shop' came alive when performed on the 2015–16 Rebel Heart Tour with—guess what?—a real car on stage. 'Body Shop' will also surely go down in history as the only Madonna song to ever mention the word 'gasket!' As was pointed out though in a number of reviews, the extended metaphor used in 'Body Shop' is incorrect as a body shop does not fix cars but generally repairs paintwork. The demo version of 'Body Shop' was a less cluttered affair with an Eastern 'wailing' backdrop.

'Holy Water'

Release: March 2015 **Album:** *Rebel Heart*
Writers: Madonna, Martin Kierszenbaum, Natalia Keery-Fisher, Mike Dean, Kanye West, Tommy Brown
Producers: Madonna, Mike Dean, Kanye West, Charlie Heat

It may not have the word bitch in its title, but 'Holy Water' is very much another default diss track ('Bitch get off my pole') and is it Yeezus (aka Kanye West), or Jesus, who 'loves my pussy best' though? During the song's climax, Madonna even pilfers her own 'Vogue' lyrics. Co-writer Kierszenbaum was then head of A&R for Madonna's label Interscope and the man who signed Lady Gaga, while Keery-Fisher is better known as Natalia Kills. For the Rebel Heart Tour version Madonna did indeed get on her pole, turning 'Holy Water' (which she insisted 'is meant to be funny') into an immaculate 'Vogue' mashup complete with half-naked nuns. She was asked to do penance by the Catholic Church for it, as you would expect.

'Inside Out'

Release: March 2015 **Album:** *Rebel Heart*
Writers: Madonna, Jason Evigan, Sean Douglas, Evan Bogart, Mike Dean
Producers: Madonna, Mike Dean

Madonna pulls us closer for a 'full disclosure' with every sin, on your knee. By insisting 'if you show me yours and I'll show you mind' it is clear her mind is in her panties again. The killer, much less dark, demo version of 'Inside Out' delivered a throbbing bassline a tad too reminiscent of Björk's 'Army of Me' from 1995, which might be why it was significantly 'readjusted'. More's the pity.

'Wash All Over Me'

Release: March 2015 **Album:** *Rebel Heart*
Writers: Madonna, Avicii, Arash Pournouri, Salem Al Fakir, Magnus Lidehall, Vincent Pontare, Mike Dean, Kanye West, Ernest Brown
Producers: Madonna, Avicii, Mike Dean, Kanye West, Charlie Heat

Was this Madonna's rumination on mortality? The leaked Avicii demo of 'Wash All Over Me' defied the final downbeat ballad version becoming a disco-house anthem and arguably the greatest Madonna song never officially released. Due to mental health issues Avicii exited *Rebel Heart* early and tragically died by his own hands three years after the release of the album, virtually prophesized in the lyrics of 'Wash All Over Me'—'Who am I to decide what should be done?/If this is the end then let it come'.

'Best Night'

Release: March 2015 **Album:** *Rebel Heart*
Writers: Madonna, Diplo, Maureen McDonald, Toby Gad, James Napier, Andrew Swanson
Producers: Madonna, Diplo

Heading into Deluxe Edition territory, the best line in 'Best Night' is undoubtedly its opener—'You can call me M tonight'. With bestie Diplo's production profoundly pirating William Orbit, 'Best Night' unfastens as a lumbering track before Madonna unexpectedly takes-off into sexily quoting 'Justify My Love' (with Ingrid Chavez again not receiving due credit). The 'Best Night' demo featured different verse lyrics about wining and dining and how Madonna is ''bout to smoke your favourite stash'. Best not to.

'Veni Vidi Vici' (Featuring Nas)

Release: March 2015 **Album:** *Rebel Heart*
Writers: Madonna, Diplo, Ariel Rechtshaid, Maureen McDonald, Toby Gad,
Nasir Jones, Joel Ma, Dustin McLean, Mark Landon
Producers: Madonna, Diplo

Time for Madonna to catalogue her own achievements—'Veni Vidi Vici'
translated from the Italian is 'I came, I saw, I conquered'—and after over thirty
years on top, why not? This is one of *Rebel Heart*'s hidden treasures with
Madonna self-referencing her catalogue from 'Holiday' onwards and giving
a welcome shout out to her most devout fanbase ('when I struck a pose/all
the gay boys lost their minds'). The blustering Nas rap, where he eviscerates
ex-wife Kelis and their 'bad divorce', almost seems to belong to a different song.
Co-writer Ma, aka Australian musician/producer Joelistics, belatedly scored a
co-writing credit with fellow Aussie McLean.

'S.E.X.'

Release: March 2015 **Album:** *Rebel Heart*
Writers: Madonna, Toby Gad, Maureen McDonald, Larry Griffin Jr, Mike
Dean, Kanye West, Ernest Brown
Producers: Madonna, Kanye West, Charlie Heat, Mike Dean

Madonna's 'back on top' here and, yes, she is talking about sex again, role-
calling all the things that get her off, including liquorice whips and latex thongs,
sandwiched between golden showers and strap-ons. Rateyourmusic.com ranked
all of the officially released *Rebel Heart* songs dumping 'S.E.X.' in last place,
calling it 'Madonna's most tin-eared attempt at eroticism since "Where Life
Begins"' (#1 was 'Ghosttown' in case you are wondering). 'S.E.X.' was one of the
few tracks from the *Rebel Heart* Deluxe/Super Deluxe Editions heard live.

'Messiah'

Release: March 2015 **Album:** *Rebel Heart*
Writers: Madonna, Avicii, Arash Pournouri, Salem Al Fakir, Magnus Lidehall,
Vincent Pontare
Producers: Madonna, Avicii, Salem Al Fakir, Magnus Lidehall, Vincent Pontare

Leaping liberally between eroticism and religious studies, *Rebel Heart*
meanders into some deep peep places and confessional booths. There's certainly
a feeling that at twenty-four tracks there needed to be some serious pruning,
while 'Messiah' is another track with overblown production blanketing some of

Madonna's most poetic lyrics ('I'll be the bride that is married to life/You are the day I am the night'). The 'Messiah' demo, however, is a dramatically beautiful piano and strings ballad, complete with chilling cinematic aura.

'Rebel Heart'

Release: March 2015 **Album:** *Rebel Heart*
Writers: Madonna, Avicii, Arash Pournouri, Salem Al Fakir, Magnus Lidehall, Vincent Pontare
Producers: Madonna, Avicii, Salem Al Fakir, Magnus Lidehall, Vincent Pontare
   Another first-rate, tough love/survivor guilt lyric by Madonna chronicles her time on earth, her choices and her reasons for them. A more chart-friendly Avicii version leaked online, demonstrating the potential and promise the album's title track had, especially as a sweeping 'Hell yeah, this is me/Right where I'm supposed to be' statement. Avicii himself preferred the demo version. Live, Madonna performed a stripped-down acoustic rendition of 'Rebel Heart' against a backdrop of fan artwork.

'Beautiful Scars'

Release: March 2015 **Album:** *Rebel Heart*
Writers: Madonna, Rick Nowels, Dacoury Natche, Michael Tucker
Producers: Madonna, DJ Dahi, Michael Diamonds
   Only found on *Rebel Heart*'s Super Deluxe Edition, a Capri disco-like setting provides the musical landscape for Madame Ciccone serenely detailing her 'stupid flaws'. That incorrigible language might actually be thanks to songwriter Nowels, previously her composer buddy on *Ray of Light*'s most tender moments. 'Beautiful Scars' is unrequitedly impassioned with a plaintive male voice (Natche/DJ Dahi) adding vocal effects, though that the over-polished released version is so different to the leaked indie guitar demo suggests Madonna struggled to get this beautifully up to scratch. In late 2020 Madonna created '#beautifulscar' when exposing the results of her hip surgery.

'Borrowed Time'

Release: March 2015 **Album:** *Rebel Heart*
Writers: Madonna, Avicii, Arash Pournouri, Carl Falk, Rami Yacoub, Savan Kotecha, Dacoury Natche, Michael Tucker
Producers: Madonna, Avicii, Falk, DJ Dahi, Michael Diamonds

'Borrowed Time' is truly like an unsolicited leftover from the *American Life* era. Madonna gets political again ('Is it all worth fighting for?'), but stuck in cliché territory, complete with acoustic guitars, wayward beats and a singalong chorus drowning in reverb. The glorious Avicii 'Borrowed Time' demo, however, is a fist-pounding, crowd-pleasing dance floor charmer that works much better than the released version.

'Addicted'

Release: March 2015 **Album:** *Rebel Heart*
Writers: Madonna, Avicii, Arash Pournouri, Carl Falk, Rami Yacoub, Savan Kotecha
Producers: Madonna, Avicii, Falk
Mad, bad, and dangerous to know goth Madonna is back ('You pulled me in/Took me down with your poisonous touch') with references to spousal abuse, addiction issues and dark heartbreak, though the chorus is trademark Avicii. His 'Addicted (The One That Got Away)' demo amped up the beats and is a helluva lot more fun. Much like the album cover itself—Madonna's face tangled up and pulled at odd angles—the material on *Rebel Heart* suffered from a lack of cohesion. The *Rebel Heart* album was indeed, as Madonna sings on 'Addicted', 'the one that got away'. In its final released form *Rebel Heart* barely sold over 1 million copies worldwide.

'Graffiti Heart'

Release: March 2015 **Album:** *Rebel Heart*
Writers: Madonna, Maureen McDonald, Toby Gad, Larry Griffin Jr
Producers: Madonna, Toby Gad, AFSHeeN, Cumbee
Madonna pays tribute to the three artists, all long since passed, who contributed much to her views on pop music, pop art, and pop culture. On the genre-hopping 'Graffiti Heart' she ruminates on the life and influences of her '80s bestie, pop artist Keith Haring, former lover and street art legend Jean-Michel Basquiat and Mexican painter Frida Kahlo. In 2019, an episode of the *Urban Myths* TV series entitled *Madonna & Basquiat* dramatized their short-lived romance (best Madonna line: 'You suck at being famous!').

'Auto-Tune Baby'

Release: March 2015 **Album:** *Rebel Heart*
Writers: Madonna, Diplo, Mike Dean, Kanye West, Ernest Brown
Producers: Madonna, Diplo, Kanye West, Mike Dean, Charlie Heat

Relegated to German versions of *Rebel Heart*, what must have started out as a studio gag—Auto-Tuning a baby crying—is proof that often what is funny in the studio is only funny in the studio. Despite questionable lyrics ('You and me sitting in a tree, you be the daddy, I'll be the baby') it is reassuring to know Madonna possesses a child-like sense of humour. Babies were also obviously weighing heavily on her mind—a year later she adopted Malawi twins, Estelle and Estere, bringing her brood to six.

21

The *Rebel Heart* Album Leaks

In late 2014, Madonna's *Rebel Heart* album not only leaked months ahead of its planned release, but so did its additional material. All up it added up to forty unique Madonna songs, many in a variety of demo versions.

That led not just to a scramble for the official release of the twenty-four songs comprising the full gamut of *Rebel Heart*'s eventual CD and digital releases, but a jail term for the Israeli hacker who accessed Madonna's laptop, stole the songs, and sold them on to a third party. Madonna described it as both 'terrorism' and 'rape'.

So, should any of the leaks, or unreleased demos, be considered 'proper' Madonna songs, should they be ignored, or do they provide a once-in-a-career chance to examine the creative process at work? In the spirit of reconciliation—and for the simple fact virtually all of the Rebel Heart demos are freely available to listen to online—here is a guide to all sixteen unreleased songs.

'Queen'

Leak: December 2014
Writers/Producers: Madonna, Mike Dean, Terius Youngdell Nash (rumoured)

Mercilessly exiled last minute from *Rebel Heart*'s international edition of the Super Deluxe Edition, 'Queen' was part of the early Deluxe Edition torrent leaks. Very much a primer for *Madame X* four years later, 'Queen' boasts a mesmeric tribal template, Madonna in strident voice, plus a woke view of the world (and is that 'The Pope' at the end blessing us all?). Why 'Queen' was banished from *Rebel Heart* remains an anti-royalist drag.

'Two Steps Behind Me'

Leak: December 2014
Writers/Producers: Madonna, Avicii (rumoured)

Was Madonna dissing Lady Gaga? That we will never know for sure, but what is certain is 'Two Steps Behind Me' is Madonna serving shade. 'You're just a wannabe me/Never gonna be me' sure sounds like a major pop beef—hold the meat dress! After this leaked, Madonna posted a contrite message insisting 'Two Steps Behind Me' was not about labelmate Lady Gaga and she did 'not wish ill towards any other female artist'. Maybe she is an apologetic bitch after all.

The other *Rebel Heart* demos

Years: 2014–2015

'Alone With You': Snide indie-pop breakup ditty reminiscent of Blondie, or her early Emmy material.

'Back That Up (Do It)': Bouncy Pharrell Williams R&B party groove later refashioned for 2019's *Madame X*.

'Freedom': Madonna back in touching heartbreak territory amid a guitar-led light rock backdrop.

'God is Love': Dramatic piano-led ballad with Madonna's plaintive vocals tackling life's big issues.

'Heaven': Emotive minimalist electronic ballad that became a firm fan favourite when it leaked.

'La Isla Bonita' (with Major Lazer): Brief studio diss track between Madonna and Diplo duly snipped from *Rebel Heart*.

'Never Let You Go': Minimalist EDM retread of earlier dance-centric hits, if not pinching from Robyn too.

'Nothing Lasts Forever': Natalia Kills co-write trumpets and updates *Ray of Light*'s lasting world music vibe.

'Revolution (Rebel Heart Tour Intro)': Talky track based around *Iconic* afforded a release on live *Rebel Heart Tour* album.

'Score': Madonna shoots for a Soccer World Cup theme with a goofball Pizzicato Five take.

'Take a Day': Fun Pharrell country/R&B hybrid as Madonna coos 'we can just bang bang bang!'

'Take It Back': Another stock R&B Pharrell production like a retro throwback to the *Hard Candy* era.

'Tragic Girl': Poignant, goosebump-inducing ballad with a very wounded sounding Madonna. Blub.

'Trust No Bitch': Bitter electro-pop rant likely about next ex, Timor Steffens, cheating on her with her PT.

22

The *Madame* X Era

Madame X
Interscope Records/Live Nation: B0030044-02
Released: June 2019
Standard Edition Tracklist

'Medellín'	4:58
'Dark Ballet'	4:14
'God Control'	6:19
'Future'	3:53
'Batuka'	4:57
'Killers Who Are Partying'	5:28
'Crave'	3:21
'Crazy'	4:02
'Come Alive'	4:02
'Faz Gostoso'	4:05
'Bitch I'm Loca'	2:50
'I Don't Search I Find'	4:08
'I Rise'	3:44

Deluxe Edition bonus tracks

'Extreme Occident'	3:41
'Looking for Mercy'	4:50

Deluxe 2-CD edition bonus tracks

'Funana'	3:42
'Back That Up to the Beat'	3:50
'Ciao Bella'	5:36

'Champagne Rosé'
(Quavo Featuring Madonna and Cardi B)

Motown/Capitol Records: B002937702 **Release:** October 2018 **Album:** *Quavo Huncho*
Writers: Quavious Marshall, Madonna, Belcalis Almanzar, Shane Lindstrom, Rasool Diaz
Producers: Murda Beatz, Quavo, Sool Got Hits

Madonna's first release as a sixty-year-old was a trap track on Quavo's debut album, *Quavo Huncho*, alongside rapper Cardi B (Almanzar). For all the talent behind this dope ode to the thrill of 'poppin' bottles', 'Champagne Rosé' falls fairly flat as Madonna, with severely treated vocals, drones, 'Please let me entertain you/ Get inside your vein to/Intoxicate your brain, ooh'. It also seemed disingenuous for previously alcohol-averse Madonna to gush about the joys of getting sloshed.

'Medellín' (Featuring Maluma)

Interscope Records/Live Nation: Digital download **Single release:** April 2019
Album: *Madame X*
Writers: Madonna, Mirwais Ahmadzaï, Juan Luis Londoño Arias (Maluma), Edgar Barrera
Producers: Madonna, Mirwais

The bilingual/Spanglish 'Medellín', a tribute to Maluma's Colombian hometown, showboated Madonna cooing risqué yet trippy lyrics, erupting sex bomb Maluma and the return of Mirwais on this trap-goes-cha-cha-cha convergence. Again, frustratingly, Madonna was hampered by her age and 'Medellín' reached a disappointing #87 in the UK—a new low for a lead Madonna single from an album. It hit #1 on the US Dance Club Chart though missing the Hot 100, her second lead album single to do so after 'Living for Love'. Yet her holographic enactment of the song with Maluma at the *Billboard Music Awards* was a timely reminder of what a great live performer Madonna is. Performed with *mucho gusto* on 2019–2020's Madame X Tour, 'Medellín' already seemed like a much-loved old friend. Ay-yi-yi!

Vid Bit!

Directors: Diana Kunst and Mau Morgó

Filmed in Madonna's newly adopted homeland of Portugal, Spanish director Kunst and visual artist Morgó gave Madonna the Latin-flavoured blockbuster, inspired by female artists Frida Kahlo and Leonora Carrington. she deserved. The chemistry between Madonna and Maluma—'slow down papi!'—was undeniably sizzling.

Remix Fix!

Offer Nissim's 'Medellín' club remakes (*Madame X in the Sphinx* and *Set Me Free*) are easily two of the best remixes of Madonna enduring career, with Nissim added to the songwriter list for his efforts. The late, great Erick Morillo also remixed *Medellín*.

'Soltera' (Maluma Featuring Madonna)

Sony Music Latin: 1907 594952 2 **Release:** May 2019 **Album:** *11:11*
Writers: Madonna, Juan Luis Londoño Arias (Maluma), Edgar Barrera, Mike Dean, Giencarlos Rivera, Jonathan Rivera
Producers: Edgar Barrera (Edge), Madmusick

Hidden away as track 10 on *11:11*, Maluma's fourth album released a month ahead of Madonna's *Madame X*, 'Soltera' ('single' in English) is light-hearted, hip-swivelling reggaeton fizz. Maluma sings in Spanish about how Madonna insists on being alone, while Madonna declares in English, with heavily treated vocals, she will not grovel for anyone, signing off carefreely with '*ciao papi*'. *11:11* eventually went double platinum in the US and Mexico and was a major hit in Spanish speaking territories, in addition to Brazil and Portugal.

'Dark Ballet'

Promo track release: June 2019 **Album:** *Madame X*
Writers/Producers: Madonna, Mirwais

Released as the second promotional track from *Madame X*, '"Dark Ballet" is an amalgamation of many different things, from Tchaikovsky to *A Clockwork Orange* to Joan of Arc,' Madonna informed *Mojo* magazine. 'When you get to the vocoder section, it's like Joan of Arc's manifesto, where she says that she will not give in and will not bow down to fear and will not apologise for what she said and she is willing to die for what she believes in. Joan of Arc was the first freedom fighter I was aware of. I can relate to her because I do fight for what I believe in.' The second song on the Madame X Tour (reversing the order with 'God Control' on the album) 'Dark Ballet' became a true piece of performance pop art.

Vid Bit!

Director: Emmanuel Adjei

Shot in Portugal, the 'Dark Ballet' video was inspired by Stanley Kubrick's 1971 dystopian film classic *A Clockwork Orange* with queer hip-hop pioneer Mykki Blanco as Joan of Arc and uncredited co-director Madonna glanced but fleetingly. A 'Director's Cut'—featuring significantly more Madonna—leaked in early 2021. Her dark response? 'DEATH TO THE PATRIARCHY!'

'God Control'

Promo track release: June 2019 **Album:** *Madame X*
Writers: Madonna, Mirwais Ahmadzaï, Casey Spooner
Producers: Madonna, Mirwais, Mike Dean

'If you're sitting alone in your apartment all day and you're writing about the downfall of humanity, it tends to get you down. After a while, you need to have fun. So, where does a girl go? She goes to a disco!' Madonna chuckled. 'I tried to bring the world of disco and freedom, and having that joy silenced by a small thing made of metal that can end someone's life.' Released as a 'promotional track' from *Madame X* after 'I Rise', 'God Control' featured the Tiffin Children's Chorus from South London's Performing Arts School. Amid swirling disco strings and a shotgun blast to bolster her anti-gun statement, 'God Control' was the opening number on Madonna's critically acclaimed Madame X Tour. Some months after *Madame X* topped the US charts, and after her tour had begun, Casey Spooner from electropop act Fischerspooner posted an excerpt of a 'God Control' demo, claiming he worked with Mirwais on the track in 2017.

Vid Bit!

Director: Jonas Åkerlund

Madonna and Åkerlund tackle gun control in the US—in the midst of a Studio 54 disco nightclub sequence—done in reverse order. Patently, the 'God Control' video is by no means subtle (spoiler alert—Madonna does not make it out alive), thus *Billboard* added it to their tally of Madonna's most controversial videos of all time.

Remix Fix!

Offer Nissim remixed and previewed 'God Control' live, with the expectation it would be the final release from *Madame X* before Madonna's tour was truncated. To date this mix has not been officially released.

'Future' (With Quavo)

Promo track release: May 2019 **Album:** *Madame X*
Writers: Madonna, Brittany Hazzard, Quavious Marshall, Thomas Pentz
Producers: Madonna, Diplo

Another of the five promotional singles from *Madame X*, 'Future' came without a video, but with a murderously Auto-unTuned major TV appearance in Tel Aviv for the *Eurovision Song Contest*. Among her many talents, no one at the time realised Madonna was also a psychic. 'Not everyone can come into the future/Not everyone that's here is gonna last' later seemed like a premonition of 2020's global lockdown. 'It's a song about the world that we live in today and the future of our civilization,' Madonna said forebodingly at the time of its release. *Madame X*'s sole Diplo production, this Jamaican dancehall track somewhat perversely, given her futuristic Israel–Palestinian coexist message at Eurovision, reached the Israeli Top 10.

'Batuka'

Promo track release: July 2019 **Album:** *Madame X*
Writers: Madonna, David Banda, Mirwais Ahmadzaï
Producers: Madonna, Mirwais
  'Batuka', referring to the Cape Verdean musical genre 'Batuque' and born from the oppressive African slave trade, is Madonna getting as close as she probably ever will to an African spiritual. Appropriately, Madonna granted her adopted African son David a co-writing credit. 'Batuka' had been mentioned early on as the album's first single, but the fact it is too unorthodox from anything Madonna has done previously, not to mention somewhat radio-unfriendly, must have swayed the powers that be to reconsider. Live and life-affirming on the Madame X Tour, 'Batuka' provided an unforgettable highlight.

VID BIT!
Director: Emmanuel Adjei
  Shot in Portugal, with Madonna donning a dark bob and featuring The Batukadeiras Orchestra, a collection of women keeping the 'Batuque' tradition alive, this spiritual, stirring, all-female video provided the perfect porthole on Madonna's newfound musical joy.

'Killers Who Are Partying'

Release: June 2019 **Album:** *Madame X*
Writers/Producers: Madonna, Mirwais
  Madonna takes on the voice/guise of a variety of persecuted minorities, or marginalized groups (in order): gays; Africans; the poor; children; Islam; Israel; Native Indians; and raped women. 'The title is really about people who are in charge, people who are in positions of power, who are doing heinous things to other people,' Madonna explained. 'Throwing people out of countries, building walls and basically doing what they consider to be their job, and then going home, or going out and having a party, having a cocktail, just acting like it's nothing,

business as usual.' As Mirwais undertakes to reinvent fado music 'Killers Who Are Partying' perks up conspicuously when Madonna switches to Portuguese. The lyrics ('The world is wild/The path is lonely') are meant to act like a fado prayer in the style of 'Queen of Morna', Cesária Évora, who died in 2011.

'Crave' (with Swae Lee)

Interscope Records/Live Nation: Digital download **Single release:** May 2019
Album: *Madame X*
Writers: Madonna, Khalif Brown, Brittany Hazzard
Producers: Madonna, Billboard, Mike Dean

Madame X's second proper single (with video) was also one of the first songs Madonna wrote for her fourteenth studio album. After putting sexy trap ballad 'Crave' on the backburner, Madonna revisited it deciding, '"I need to sing with a man on this!" It's a song about desire and longing,' and hauled in Swae Lee. Although *Crave* did well on *Billboard*'s Adult Contemporary Chart (serviced to radio as a solo Madonna track) it failed to crack the US Hot 100 chart, also bypassing the UK Top 100. On the Madame X Tour, Madonna performed the Tracy Young Dangerous Remix transforming 'Crave' into a party thang. Spotify playlisters might best position Madonna's thirsty 'Crave' alongside earlier heartfelt R&B hankerings like 1994's 'Secret' and 2015's 'Inside Out.

VID BIT!
Director: Nuno Xico

The 'Crave' video, complete with Swae, NYC homing pigeons and an ageless Madonna was suitably stylish and bewitching, yet callously ignored by the mainstream. Due to the success of 'Crave' in the clubs, the clip was recut to the Tracy Young Dangerous Remix including Madonna's additional dialogue.

REMIX FIX!
MNEK, Tracy Young, Benny Benassi, RNG, Otto Benson, Twisted D & Diego Fernandez, Dan De Leon & Anthony Griego, Thomas Gold, DJLW, Boris, Mike Cruz and Joe Gauthreaux & Leanh were the dirty dozen remixers brought to the 'Crave' cave.

'Crazy'

Release: June 2019 **Album:** *Madame X*
Writers: Madonna, Jason Evigan, Brittany Hazzard
Producers: Madonna, Mike Dean, Jason Evigan

Like 'Crave', 'Crazy' also harks back to the softer, cosier R&B stylings of 1994's *Bedtime Stories*. Besides its Portuguese musical journey and politically woke lyrics, *Madame X*'s other great rediscovery is that of joy. After the pre-divorce *Hard Candy*, post-divorce *MDNA* and lonely *Rebel Heart*, it is not churlish to declare *Madame X* is Madonna's most exuberant album since 2000's *Music*. All that wonder of discovery, life and love were succinctly encapsulated when 'Crazy' was enthrallingly performed live in a recreated Portuguese backstreet fado cafe on the Madame X Tour.

'Come Alive'

Release: June 2019 **Album:** *Madame X*
Writers: Madonna, Jeff Bhasker, Brittany Hazzard
Producers: Madonna, Jeff Bhasker, Mike Dean
'Come Alive' is a jaunty, catchy, lively track which might even have succeeded in bridging the ample gap between Beyoncé and Ariana Grande. Bhasker and Madonna definitely need to make more beautiful music together like this in the future. After *Madame X* he worked on Harry Styles' sophomore album and someone Madonna would levitate to next, Dua Lipa.

'Faz Gostoso' (Featuring Anitta)

Release: June 2019 **Album:** *Madame X*
Writers: Madonna, Rodrigo Carmo, Duarte Nuno, Emanuel Oliveira, Mateus Seabra, Luiz Vieira, Karla Rodrigues
Producers: Madonna, Billboard, Mike Dean
'Faz Gostoso' was previously a Portuguese #1 for Brazilian singer Blaya (aka Rodrigues), but Madonna's version features another Brazilian singer, Anitta. 'Faz Gostoso' translates as 'so yummy' in all senses, including sexual, with Madonna added as co-writer, likely thanks to the 'losing your mind' English lyric. The frenetic beat, spicy lyrics and deft mix of languages fuses 'Faz Gostoso' into a truly delectable pansexual duet. 'Being by your side is a lifelong learning,' Anitta said of her tasty collaborator, 'endless gratitude.'

'Bitch I'm Loca' (Featuring Maluma)

Release: June 2019 **Album:** *Madame X*
Writers: Madonna, Lauren D'Elia, Juan Luis Londoño Arias (Maluma), Edgar Barrera, George James, Marvin Rodriguez, Stiven Rojas
Producers: Madonna, Billboard, Sunamy

Madonna did not record two songs with Colombian heartthrob rapper Maluma she laid down three. 'Bitch I'm Loca' is debatably the lesser of their collaborations. As Madonna crows 'I like to be on top' the frisky reggaeton beat carries the song before reaching its zenith when Maluma asks Madonna where he should put it. 'Inside!' she titters. A suitable wacky companion to 1990's 'I'm Going Bananas'.

'I Don't Search I Find'

Interscope Records/Live Nation: Digital download **Single release:** December 2019 **Album:** *Madame X*
Writers/Producers: Madonna, Mirwais

The fifth promotional single from *Madame X* is arguably the most 'trad Madonna' of anything on this wildly eclectic album as she zips up her boots and goes back to her roots! 'I Don't Search I Find' steals inspiration from 'Vogue' as an old school Madonna pop house track, with a nod also to 1990's oft-overlooked 'Rescue Me'. Critically *Madame X* garnered Madonna's best reviews in two decades with *NME*, *Billboard*, *Slant Magazine*, *Idolator*, and *Albumism* listing it as one of 2019's fifty best albums. *The New York Post* chose 'I Don't Search I Find' as the eighth best song of 2019.

Remix Fix!

No chances were taken ensuring 'I Don't Search I Find' scored Madonna her record-breaking fiftieth US Dance Club Song #1. In May 2020, a digital EP of 'I Don't Search I Find' remixes (minus Honey Dijon's awe-inspiring dubby revisions) was issued in memory of dance music specialist/Madonna champion Orlando Puerta who died from COVID-19. In July 2021, a Honey Dijon dub mix soundtracked Madonna's 'No Fear, Courage, Resist' video art installation to support the LGBTQ community, later wildly performing Dijon's 'IDSIF' remix live, plus club staples 'Hung Up' and 'Vogue', for NYC Pride.

'I Rise'

Interscope Records/Live Nation: B0031093-11 **12″ release:** May 2019 **Album:** *Madame X*
Writers: Madonna, Brittany Talia Hazzard (Starrah), Jason Evigan
Producers: Madonna, Jason Evigan

'I Rise' was released after 'Medellín' as the first promotional single from *Madame X*. It not only closed the *Madame X* album, but was also the song Madonna chose to end her short, but historic, set at the *Stonewall 50: WorldPride NYC 2019* concert, as well being the encore song for her Madame

X Tour. Sampling US school shooting survivor Emma Gonzalez: 'Us kids don't know what we're talking about/That we're too young to understand how the government works/We call B.S.' Madonna wrote 'I Rise', 'as a way of giving a voice to all marginalised people who feel they don't have the opportunity to speak their mind'. Stirring stuff and of all of *Madame X*'s punts at a political agenda the one that seemed most cohesive and, at 3:44 minutes, most concise.

VID BIT!
Director: Peter Matkiwsky

A Madonna video without Madonna? Yep, that finally happened with this powerful, politically charged social justice clip, put together with footage from *TIME* Studios' archives.

VIVA VINYL!
A 'Black Friday' Record Store Day release of a 12″ vinyl single was distributed, primarily in the US. A total 4,000 copies were reportedly pressed.

REMIX FIX!
Tracy Young's Pride Remix—celebrating the fiftieth anniversary of the Stonewall riots that led to gay liberation movements and later LGBT+ rights—won Best Remixed Recording at the 62nd Grammy Awards in early 2020.

'Extreme Occident'

Release: June 2019 **Album:** *Madame X*
Writers/Producers: Madonna, Mirwais

One of the two extra tracks on *Madame X*'s Deluxe Edition, the poetic, stirring 'Extreme Occident' was influenced by Cape Verde's national music called Morna. 'I'm saying I'd been told I was lost, I was confused and I didn't really know what I was talking about,' Madonna told *Mojo* magazine. 'I paid for the things I said and did and spoke out against, or fought for, and I listened to too many people telling me that I was wrong, or that I should be quiet, that I should go away … I should have just listened to my voice and believed in myself.'

'Looking for Mercy'

Release: June 2019 **Album:** *Madame X*
Writers: Madonna, Brittany Hazzard
Producers: Madonna, Jeff Bhasker, Mike Dean

The album's other 'bonus' track heralds the return of compelling balladeer Madonna. 'Looking for Mercy' might be both a lullaby for daughter Mercy, or a plea by Madonna to the divine 'to forgive myself'. With its stirring entreaty to 'teach me about love', more so than any other song 'Looking for Mercy' channels *Madame X*'s, if not Madonna's, recurring theme of struggling with loneliness in a world where love is hard to find. 'Looking for Mercy' was mercilessly omitted from her Madame X Tour. Looking ahead, Madonna returned to the studio with Dean in early 2022.

'Funana'

Release: June 2019 **Album:** *Madame X*
Writers/Producers: Madonna, Mirwais
Three tracks—'Funana', 'Back That Up to the Beat', and 'Ciao Bella'—completed *Madame X*'s Deluxe 2-CD Box Set. 'Let's go dancing!' Madonna at last implores, so *Funana* is truly the album's official afterhours party. Madonna proceeds to give shout outs to music legends since passed—Elvis Presley, Bob Marley, Whitney Houston, James Brown, Aretha Franklin, George Michael, David Bowie, Tupac Shakur, Avicii, Mac Miller, Freddie Mercury, and Prince. No Michael Jackson? Shady! The 'Funana' title refers to an accordion-based style of music/dance from Africa's Cape Verde islands, though little of that is truly discernible here.

'Back That Up to the Beat'

Release: June 2019 **Album:** *Madame X*
Writers: Madonna, Pharrell Williams, Brittany Hazzard
Producers: Madonna, Jeff Bhasker, Mike Dean, Pharrell Williams
Originally a leaked leftover from the *Rebel Heart* sessions, this song floated around in demo form for years. All that remains from the original Williams production are the lyrics and basic melody. Musically, 'Back That Up to the Beat' has been significantly souped up with spacey synths, Afrocentric drumbeats and Madonna's voice transmitted in from another dimension.

'Ciao Bella'

Release: June 2019 **Album:** *Madame X*
Writers/Producers: Madonna, Mirwais
Over a moody, if melancholy, house beat Madonna offers a rare peek into her conflicted headspace ('Sometimes I despair, sometime I have hope/Sometimes I don't know, sometimes I feel happy'). Performed with Dino D'Santiago,

Madonna told French magazine *Têtu,* 'he was kind of an interface. He is from Cape Verde and most of the musicians from Cape Verde I worked with don't speak English.' One of the most personal tracks from the album 'Ciao Bella' ushers *Madame X* off the stage with her final words being the symbolic, 'All the noise just disappears, rain will wash away the sadness/All our lives we work in vain, for a little touch of grace'.

'Levitating'
(Dua Lipa Featuring Madonna & Missy Elliott)

Warner Music: Digital download **12″ Vinyl Release:** August 2020 **Album:** *Club Future Nostalgic: The Remix Album*
Writers: Clarence Coffee Jr, Dua Lipa, Sarah Hudson, Stephen Kozmeniuk, Madonna, Melissa A. Elliott
Producers: Koz, Stuart Price **Remixer:** The Blessed Madonna

After curtailing her Madame X Tour due to a knee injury and COVID-19 (later testing positive for the antibodies), during 2020 Madonna took time out to convalesce, nurse a heavy social media addiction, and toil on a screenplay about her origins with Oscar winner Diablo Cody. Released two days before her sixty-second birthday, the bass-pumping 'Levitating' collab with Dua Lipa, Missy Elliott, and remix/producer The Blessed Madonna (formerly The Black Madonna) was, to quote *Billboard,* 'nothing short of epic'. The 'hella cute' 'Levitating' returned her to the world's pop singles charts and notably marked the first time Madonna and Price had been together on a record since 2008. Importantly, 'Levitating' saw Madonna return to her original label of Warner Music after her three-album deal with Interscope ended. Almost forty years later, Madonna's 'starlight' remained star bright. *Billboard* ranked 'Levitating' as 2021's #1 song overall.

VID BIT!
Director: Will Hooper

Although this timely, non-binary, inclusive, love conquers all, kitchen disco clip included celestial beings, skaters, and glowing crystals—plus a flashy Missy Elliott cameo—there is nary a sign of Madonna. A radiant, sexy, and scene-stealing Lipa, nonetheless, certainly gave credence to the notion she might eventually be Madonna's natural successor to the Queen of Pop title.

REMIX FIX!
Dance and sing! Just like 'Everybody', Madonna's first release almost forty years earlier, a 12″ of 'Levitating' on The Blessed Madonna's label We Still Believe was issued.

Material Girl Gone Wild—
The Extra Extras!

Essential demos, mixes, rarities, live tracks and additional soundtrack recordings!

1979

'Let the Sunshine In' (a #1 1969 hit from the *Hair* musical briefly sung by Madonna on the soundtrack to the student horror film *A Certain Sacrifice*).

'She's a Real Disco Queen' (written and produced by Belgian Jean Vanloo for then *protégé* Madonna to record. After touring and a Dutch TV appearance on *TopPop* with Vanloo hit maker Patrick Hernandez, promoting his 'Born to Be Alive' global disco hit, Madonna fled Paris back to New York. Hernandez later had a minor hit with 'Disco Queen', which could be 'She's a Real Disco Queen').

THE GILROY TAPES DEMOS AKA THE BREAKFAST CLUB (MADONNA ON LEAD VOCALS)

'Born to Be a Dancer' (brief excerpt of this post-punk guitar tune).

'Over and Over' (very early version of track later on 1984's *Like a Virgin* album).

'Tell the Truth' (Madonna sang this during a UK TV interview on *Parkinson* claiming it was the first song she ever wrote. A one-minute excerpt leaked in June 2020).

'I Got Trouble (Roll Over It)' (another punky rock tune).

'Nobody Wants to Be Alone' (Madonna gets needy on this bluesy rock number).

'Trouble' (more punk thrash with Madonna's vocals reminiscent of Lene Lovich).

'Well Well' (a cutesy looping ditty insisting 'move it along/I cannot be late tonight').

'Baby Come Home' (Madonna sings poignantly about getting a letter from her father).

'The Sky is Blue' (unplugged strummed electric guitar about heading to the rooftop).

'Oh Oh (The Sky is Blue)' (garage band-style effort running under two minutes).

'Little Boy Lost' (fast-paced B-52's inspired demo written by Madonna and Gilroy).

'No Running in the City', 'All My Love', 'On the Ground' (other titles mentioned as existing during this period but unconfirmed and no leaks to date if so).

1980

EMMY AND THE EMMYS DEMOS (MADONNA ON LEAD VOCALS)

'(I Like) Love for Tender' (a polished studio version with Madonna in fine vocal form on this four-track official demo recorded in November, 1980 in New York City).

'No Time for Love' (less post-punk and more new wave that recalls Blondie-lite).

'Bells Ringing' (jangly '60s-esque rock tune with Madonna's voice ringing out brashly).

'Drowning' (early '80s new wave with synth flourishes and Madonna singing stridently).

'Love Express' (guitars aplenty track about getting the 'love express to your address).

'Safe Neighborhood' (Madonna shouts her lyrics in true shit-stirring punk style).

'Burning Up' (a Blondie-like punk-rock demo version of the classic Madonna single).

'Shine a Light' (girl-group-meets-post-punk number that first surfaced on a bootleg picture disc in Europe in 1992, then leaked in 2009).

1981

1ST TIME OUT OF MANHATTAN—EMMY & THE EMMYS LIVE RECORDINGS (MADONNA ON LEAD VOCALS)

'Best Girl' (thrashy post-punk pop with Madonna declaring 'I'll be your best girl, baby!' from 1994's unofficial bootleg *1st Time Out of Manhattan* album).

'Hot House Flower' (more noisy, sweaty guitar rock that demonstrates early promise).

'Bells Ringing' (rock stomper announcing the world's end with Madonna in fine voice).

'Simon Says' (not-so-spectacular raucous '60s-like guitar rock).

'Nobody's Fool' (Madonna called this duelling guitar track 'everyone's theme song').

'No Time for Love' (moshpit staple nod to Blondie's 1979 'Union City Blue' hit).

'Drowning' (another convergence of post-punk new wave rock that's very Blondie).

'Love for Tender' (another recording of this rock track with amended title).

'Love Express' (another recording of this punky pop track—fun to pogo to).

The Gotham Tapes (solo recordings for then manager Camille Barbone)

'Get Up' (final demo pointing to the new wave dance-pop direction Madonna would gravitate to, complete with her first stab at rapping. After almost thirty years in legal hell 'Get Up' finally leaked in 2009).

'Take Me (I Want You)' (a song that cannot decide if it is sweet pop or angsty punk).

'Love On the Run' (catchy ska number with an unshakeable chorus).

'High Society (Society's Boy)' (Madonna 'invents' synth-grunge—an early highlight).

The Media Sound Tapes

'Are You Ready for It?' (punky guitars and a strong pop hook that leaked in 2012).

'Remembering Your Touch' (another lesser demo that also leaked in 2012).

Otto Von Wernherr (Madonna on backing vocals)

'Cosmic Climb', 'We Are the Gods', 'Wild Dancing' (three songs credited to German artist Otto Von Wernherr for whom Madonna contributed backing vocals. After her meteoric rise to fame, Von Wernherr remixed his sinister-synth Europop dirges in 1986 to make Madonna more prominent, splashing her image on the covers to cash in on her success. A further slew of tracks—'Shake', 'Oh My!', 'On the Street', 'Get Down', 'Give It to Me', 'Let's Go Dancing', and 'Time to Dance (Time and Time Again)'—containing variations of the same vocals were recycled until at least 1992).

In the Beginning/Pre-Madonna aka the Stephen Bray Tapes

Almost a decade after he finished working with Madonna, Stephen Bray plundered his archives for a Soultone album release in 1997 of ten demos from 1980–1981 he appeared to own the rights to. Of tracks previously released on Madonna records, 'Ain't No Big Deal' appeared in three versions, 'Everybody' got two, plus 'Stay' and 'Burning Up'. All tracks, bar 'Ain't No Big Deal', which Bray wrangled sole credit for, were written by Madonna.

'Crimes of Passion' (more fluffy pop than dirty punk written with David Frank, later a member of The System, who reworked the song as 'It's Passion').

'Don't You Know?' (Madonna gets her electrofunk street groove on here).

'Laugh to Keep from Crying' (indie rock, Pretenders-like track).

1982

'We Live In a House' (unleaked demo by Spinal Root Gang written by Josh Braun, Madonna and her then roommate Janice Galloway).

'Shake Your Head (Let's Go to Bed)' (recorded by Was (Not Was) featuring Madonna, Carol Hall and Ozzy Osbourne. Due to her Sire contract, Madonna's vocals were removed. A 1992 remix featuring actress Kim Basinger reached #4 in the UK, with Madonna's version finally leaking in full in 2008).

1983

'Promises Promises' (US #11 hit by British electropop duo Naked Eyes remixed by Madonna's then boyfriend Jellybean with his girlfriend on backing vocals).

1984

'Like a Virgin' (writers' demo—finally the heterosexual male version of Madonna's classic).

'Crazy for You' (writers' demo—sung by a male voice and with a much more country rock influence).

'Warning Signs' (synth-pop track intended for the *Vision Quest* movie which was cut. Although this track has not leaked to date, oddly enough its lyrics appear to have).

'Desperately Seeking Susan' (lost second demo for Madonna's 1985 movie).

'Into the Groove' (demo—used on the *Desperately Seeking Susan* soundtrack).

1985

'Like a Virgin' (The Virgin Tour mashup of Michael Jackson's 1983 'Billie Jean' hit).

1986

'Pipeline/I Want You' (two reported Stephen Bray demos).

'Work Your Fingers to the Bone' (in 2016 Jellybean announced he had 'just found' a final mix of this unreleased Madonna track intended for a musical called *Street Smarts*. To date it has been neither been released nor leaked).

'Open Your Heart' (writers' demo—co-writer Peter Rafelson gives his original male take on this Madonna classic. Another demo featuring credited co-writer Gardner Cole's girlfriend Donna De Lory has been spotted intermittently online).

'Each Time You Break My Heart' (Madonna demo—see separate entry in Chapter 3).

1987

'Tell Me' (underrated Nick Kamen single written by Patrick Leonard and Kamen with Madonna on backing vocals. Stephen Bray reportedly confirmed a Madonna demo of 'Tell Me' exists).

'Spotlight' (writers' demo—excerpts of track, possibly sung by 'Holiday' co-writer Lisa Stevens).

1988

'Scheherazade' (overwrought track from Peter Cetera's *One More Story* album produced/co-written by Patrick Leonard. Madonna, as Lulu Smith, contributes vocals).

'Like a Prayer'/'Cherish' (in 2019, Patrick Leonard uploaded the original demos of both songs as a way of stopping fans bidding on a cassette of unreleased recordings being auctioned by Madonna's former art adviser Darlene Lutz. While 'Cherish' is close to the released version, 'Like a Prayer' features what became the final vocal and Madonna as her own multitracked heavenly gospel configuration. Leonard also uploaded 'Angels With Dirty Faces' (see entry in Chapter 5) and images of a ten-track demo cassette from the *Like a Prayer* sessions with the names of two unreleased instrumentals, 'Bossa Nova' and '20s Jazz', he called 'sparks that made no fire').

'First is a Kiss' (one of two tracks co-written with Stephen Bray that did not make the cut because they didn't fit the mood of the record, according to Bray).

'Love Attack' (another nixed Stephen Bray track, both of which remain unleaked).

'Possessive Love' (pedestrian synth-pop track performed by Marilyn Martin, written by Madonna, Jai Winding and Patrick Leonard and co-produced by Leonard. The lyrical content of 'Possessive Love'—'letting go is the hardest part'—may have hit too close to home at the time as Madonna contemplated reconciling/divorcing husband Sean Penn).

'Just a Dream' (another 'divorce' song, written by Madonna and Patrick Leonard during *Like A Prayer*, given to backing singer Donna De Lory for a minor hit in 1993)

1989

'I Surrender Dear' (cute flapper ballad duet by Madonna with Jennifer Grey on this 1931 Bing Crosby classic from ensemble period comedy *Bloodhounds of Broadway*).

'I Got You Babe' (ditzy cover of Sonny & Cher hit at *Don't Bungle the Jungle* concert with fleeting 'twinsie' Sandra Bernhard).

1990

'To Love You' (written with Andy Paley for *I'm Breathless* but cut. A listing for this title exists, but though the demo was re-recorded in 1994 neither version has leaked).

'Dog House' (likely to be Madonna's version of 'You're In the Doghouse Now' written by Andy Paley for the *Dick Tracy* soundtrack which Brenda Lee recorded).

'Get Over' (Madonna/Stephen Bray co-write—see entry in Chapter 8).

Blond Ambition (Los Angeles Rehearsals—fourteen tracks including a version of 'Vogue' called 'Non Vocal Demo' and 'Into the Groove' sampling Inner City's 'Ain't Nobody Better' 1989 hit).

'Holiday' (*Blond Ambition* version featuring elements of The Fatback Band's 1975 disco nugget '(Are You Ready) Do the Bus Stop)'.

'Keep It Together' (*Blond Ambition* version featuring elements of Sly and The Family Stone's 'Family Affair' classic from 1971).

'Rock the Vote' (campy political public service announcement done as an *a cappella* take on 'Vogue' ending with Madonna decreeing 'and if you don't vote you're going to get a spanking!').

1992

'You Are the One' (bass-heavy pop-house demo chopped from *Erotica*. Leaked in 2014).

'Shame' (demo cut from *Erotica*. 'What a shame Shame wasn't released!' Pettibone tartly noted).

'Jitterbug' (cute Pettibone/Shimkin demo intended for the A League of Their Own soundtrack. A brief excerpt leaked in 2019).

'Actions Speak Louder Than Words' (dancier Pettibone/Shimkin demo of 'Words' from Erotica that finally leaked in 2019).

'Cheat (Drunk Girl)' (early 'Bad Girl' demo uncannily like the finished version—is it a fake?—that 'leaked' in 2019).

'Dear Father' (above average pop-dance demo co-written by Andre Betts and Mic Murphy from The System cut from Erotica but finally leaked in 2008).

'Love Hurts' (early version of 'Erotica' with a different chorus and lyrics—'I'll hit you like a Mack truck'—produced by Junior Vasquez and leaked in 2017).

'You Thrill Me' (less polished Shep Pettibone version of Erotica leaked in 2008).

1993

'The Lady is a Tramp' (Madonna covers the Rodgers & Hart showtune with Red Hot Chili Peppers' Anthony Kiedis on the 1,000th episode of The Arsenio Hall Show).

1994

'Goodtime', 'Tongue Tied', 'Bring It' (three reported Shep Pettibone demos that have not leaked).

'Right On Time' (Dallas Austin demo cut from Bedtime Stories that has not leaked).

'Love Won't Wait' (topflight Madonna/Pettibone tune given to Take That's Gary Barlow and released as his first UK solo single where it hit #1 in 1997. Madonna's charming, if unpolished, lo-fi, Motown-inspired demo leaked some years later).

'Something's Coming Over Me' (original demo of 'Secret' with Shep Pettibone—who would later demand, and receive, a co-writing credit—that has not leaked).

'I Will Always Have You' (original Shep Pettibone demo of what became 'Inside of Me' on Bedtime Stories. Leaked briefly before abruptly disappearing).

'Secret' ('cyberheads' internet promo version with message from Madonna— 'welcome to the 90s version of intimacy'—and a running time of 6:42).

1995

'I Can't Forget' (see 'One More Chance' entry in Chapter 10).

'You'll See' (Spanglish Version #2—released on promo only).

Japanese Takara TV commercial for Jun Legend sake (thirty-second piece of music reportedly taken from a demo called 'Indian Summer' that has not leaked to date).

'Singing Telegram' (Madonna's cameo as Telegram girl from her Blue in the Face movie).

1996

'If Madonna Calls' (from this brief phone message a vengeful Junior Vasquez— Madonna reportedly let him down for a club performance—created a bitch track of 'queens reading queens' that went to #24 in the UK and #2 on the US dance charts).

1997

'Fantasy' (and he was not finished yet! Another Junior Vasquez dance production, credited to Race Featuring Who's Dat Girl?, there is a suggestion its origins are from a derivative Enigma-esque demo from the early Erotica sessions with a singer insisting 'I'll be your fantasy'. In their 1997 review of 'Fantasy' Billboard magazine conceded Who's Dat Girl? 'sounds a tiny bit like Madonna').

Evita—Work In Progress or the Evita Sessions (early studio versions that leaked including demos of 'Don't Cry for Me Argentina' and an a cappella of 'You Must Love Me').

'I'll Be Gone' (plodding Babyface demo that finally leaked in 2019).

'Never Love a Stranger' (another laboured Babyface demo which leaked in 2019).

1998

'No Substitute for Love' (early version of 'Drowned World/Substitute for Love').

'Gone Gone Gone' (perky yet bleak demo written by Madonna and Rick Nowells).

'Revenge' (poetic pop demo written by Madonna, Greg Fitzgerald and Rick Nowels recorded in 2001 by UK popstress Sophie Ellis-Bextor, but Madonna's moody, mystical deep house version finally leaked in 2009).

'Like a Flower' (plaintive ballad demo, written about her mother with Rick Nowells. Released in 2004 by Laura Pausini in Italian as 'Mi abbandono a te' and in Spanish as 'Me Abandono A Ti').

'You'll Stay' (possibly an earlier incarnation of 'Like a Flower', which leaked in 2019).

'Flirtation Dance' ('eastern/Indian' version of 'Skin' produced by Patrick Leonard, which leaked in 2019).

'Regresando' (reported Patrick Leonard demo that has not yet leaked).

2000

'Like an Angel Passing through My Room' (see separate listing in Chapter 17).

'Liquid Love' (pulsating Orbit demo rejected from Music sneakily mixed with an instrumental of David Guetta's 'When Love Takes Over').

'Little Girl' (sweet ballad demo, clearly directed at daughter Lourdes, cut from Music).

'La Petite Jeune Fille' (alternate take of 'Little Girl' with typical Orbit dance backing that leaked in 2011).

'Alone Again' (Madonna/Rick Nowells demo given to Kylie Minogue who used it for her 2007 White Diamond documentary. Madonna's demo remains unleaked).

'Arioso' (flute-based Orbit demo became the Wonderland TV series score).

'Wonderland' (instrumental track used as the theme for the two existing episodes of the Wonderland TV series. This leaked a decade later).

'Mysore Smile' (Orbit demo about Indian city of Mysore possibly recycled for 'La Petite Jeune Fille').

'Run' ('60s guitar-pop electronica Orbit demo rejected from Music album).

'The Music's No Good Without You' (reported demo that has not leaked to date).

2001

'The Funny Song' (goofy barnyard singalong performed live on Drowned World Tour).

2002

'Come On to My House' (sung by Della Reese and the only two minutes in Swept Away you need to see in this dream sequence where Madonna lip syncs for her life).

2003

'Can't You See My Mind' (rumoured second track for Die Another Day soundtrack that has not leaked),

The English Roses (Madonna as children's author? Listen and believe, kids! For a giggle google the French & Saunders parody with Dawn French as Madonna/Esther).

'It's So Cool' (early demos—see separate listing in Chapter 18).

'The Game' (leaked Mirwais folkie-protest demo rejected from American Life).

'To the Left, To the Right' (Mirwais libertarian guitar-electronica demo rejected from American Life that also leaked as 'Set the Right').

'I'm In Love with Love' (Mirwais grrl-rock demo rejected from American Life leaked in 2010).

'Miss You' (guitar strumming Mirwais demo rejected from American Life leaked in 2010).

'React' (reported Mirwais demo rejected from American Life).

2004

'If You Go Away' (melodramatic leaked piano demo of Jacques Brel/Rod McKuen tearjerker recorded for the aborted Hello Suckers musical).

'Is This Love (Bon D'Accord)' (dramatic leaked demo from Hello Suckers).

'Boum!' (cutesy Hello Suckers cover of Charles Trenet's 1938 French classic that leaked in 2015).

'Curtain' (reported Hello Suckers demo).

2005

'Imagine' (brooding live version from 2004's Re-invention World Tour released by the UK's Q Magazine on Lennon Covered #2 bonus CD).

In mid-2020, a group of Madonna fans bandied together to cough up a reported £1,500 to purchase a set of nine Madonna Confessions demos—'Hung Up', 'Sorry', 'Jump', 'I Love New York', 'Forbidden Love', 'History', 'Push', 'Funny Game', and 'Fighting Spirit (Instrumental)'—being sold on the black market. While 'Hung Up', 'Jump', 'Forbidden Love', and 'Push' closely resemble the finished versions, of most interest is 'Sorry' featuring significantly different verses ('the lonely days are gone/ I'm finally moving on'), a noticeably dancier 'I Love New York' and 'Funny Game', a minimalist early take on album leftover 'Super Pop' (see entry in Chapter 16).

'Triggering Your Senses' (clumpy Mirwais demo rejected from Confessions that leaked in 2010).

'Queen of Hearts' (reported demo that has not leaked).

2006

'Feel Good Inc vs Hung Up' (well hung Gorillaz/Madonna holographic Grammy Awards mashup).

'Come Closer' (cool retitled cover by electronic act Tilt of 1995's 'I Can't Forget' demo originally co-written by Madonna with David Foster for Something to Remember).

'Imagine' (live version of John Lennon classic released on I'm Going to Tell You a Secret album).

2007

'She's Madonna' (snappy Robbie Williams single co-written and produced by Pet Shop Boys based on a conversation Williams had with then girlfriend Tania Strecker on why her ex-boyfriend, Guy Ritchie, left her. The song peaked at #16 in the UK).

2008

'I Can't Forget' (slushy cover by Italian/Canadian singer Angelica Di Castro of Madonna's unused demo from Something to Remember).

'Across the Sky' (terrific demo featuring Justin Timberlake produced by Timbaland rejected from Hard Candy that leaked).

'Animal' (formulaic Timbaland demo rejected from Hard Candy which leaked).

'Infinity' (leaked pre-Pharrell Williams demo version of 'Give It 2 Me').

'La La (Latte)' (aka 'Pala Tute (The Madness of Love)' a demo by Madonna, Justin Timberlake, Gogol Bordello, Danja, and Timbaland rejected from Hard Candy. Later sung during the Sticky & Sweet Tour and at Live Earth).

'The Beat is So Crazy' (Pharrell Williams demo cut from Hard Candy. A duet version with Eve leaked some years later).

'Silly Girl' (demo—reported track that has not leaked).

2009

'The Sweet Machine/Candy Shop' (live recording from Sticky & Sweet Tour).

'Rain/Here Comes the Rain Again' (live recording mashing in Eurythmics hit from Sticky & Sweet Tour).

'Doli Doli' (trad-gypsy song performed live on Sticky & Sweet Tour by Kolpakov Trio).

2009

'Broken' (acoustic version with Madonna fluffing at the beginning which leaked in 2011).

'Just Too Tall' (duet with rapper Lil' Kim that remains unverified. Is it just a tall tale?).

2010

'The Sweet Machine' (concert video opener from Sticky & Sweet Tour live DVD).

2012

'Bang Bang Boom' (Mika demo, which became 'Gang Bang', leaked in various forms, including with co-writer Priscilla Renea on vocals and an instrumental demo).

'Give It To Me' (mashed-up with special live guest Psy and his 'Gangnam Style' hit in NYC).

2013

'Same Love' (Madonna warbles 'Open Your Heart' excerpt during Macklemore & Ryan Lewis's Grammy Awards performance).

'Je T'aime Moi Non Plus' ('naughty' '60s French hit by Serge Gainsbourg and Jane Birkin sung live in Paris during the MDNA one-off promo tour that streamed online).

'Virgin Mary (Intro)' (the opening number on the MDNA Tour).

'America (My Country 'Tis of Thee)' (patriotic American song sung by Madonna during her secretprojectrevolution art film).

2015

'La Vie en rose' (live recording of Edith Piaf classic hit with Madonna on ukulele).

'If I Had a Hammer' (cover of the 1950 folk protest song used during the Rebel Heart Tour as a backdrop and never officially released).

2016

'Nothing Compares 2 U'/'Purple Rain' (ill-advised Madonna tribute to Prince with Stevie Wonder at Billboard Music Awards).

'Highlights' (typically moody Kanye West track featuring Madonna vocals which leaked in lo-fi. The version on West's The Life of Pablo album axed Madonna).

'Send in the Clowns' (cover of Stephen Sondheim's classic at Tears of a Clown show).

'Between the Bars' (originally from Elliott Smith's 1997 album and performed at the same TOAC show. Madonna also performed 'Between the Bars' in 2013 at a screening of her secretprojectrevolution short film with son Rocco as a masked dancer. In 2017, she posted a version from her home on Instagram).

'Toxic' (cover of Britney Spears's 2004 hit sung during Miami's Tears of a Clown show).

2018

'Beautiful Game' (later to become 'Dark Ballet', debuted at The MET Gala, alongside 'Like a Prayer' and a cover of Leonard Cohen's 'Hallelujah').

2019

'Fado Pechincha' (cover of Portuguese folk classic made famous by the late Celeste Rodrigues, performed with her great-grandson Gaspar Varela during Madame X Tour).

'Sodade' (cover of 1950s Cape Verdean coladeira song, made famous by Cesária Évora, sung with Cape Verdean artist Dino d'Santiago on Madame X Tour).

2020

'I'm Dreaming' (one of a number of very early, very raw, 1980s demos Madonna posted of herself online listening to for inspiration for her forthcoming biopic).

'Burning Up' (excerpt from original demo of her 1983 hit that Madonna uploaded to celebrate the win of Joe Biden/Kamala Harris in the US Presidency race).

2021

'Gang Signs' (Madonna aka 'Muff Daddy' puffs but does not sing in Snoop Dogg feat. Mozzy's dope beat video where he raps blissfully about 'passing joints to Madonna').

In a Guardian interview, Mirwais revealed his third album, The Retrofuture, due 2022, would contain superstar contributions. That concurred with Madonna previously posting, 'This is NOT my new music.... But I'm having fun in the studio inbetween takes'. She then, not so cryptically, hashtagged Mirwais. Madame neXt?

Madonna was also spotted in the studio with The Weeknd's co-manager/producer Amir 'Cashxo' Esmailian, though this may be related to her boyfriend, Ahlamalik Williams, recording under the name of SKITZO.

Reports, true blue or otherwise, circulated Madonna was reuniting with Patrick Leonard for her upcoming biopic causing long-time fans to become truly breathless with anticipation.

On Madonna's sixty-third birthday (16 August 2021, of course), it was announced she had returned to Warner Music in a deal that sees her three non-Warner albums, MDNA, Rebel Heart, and Madame X, become part of the Warner catalogue from 2025. Even better news was Warner Music's plans for an extensive multi-year series of catalogue reissues, with Madonna personally curating deluxe editions and unique releases for special events, with 'much more' promised. What was missed by most, however, was the deal covers seventeen studio albums—meaning Madonna effectively owed three new ones. 'I am delighted to be embarking on this next chapter with (Warner Music Group) to celebrate my catalogue from the last 40 years,' Madonna declared ahead of the fortieth anniversary of her recording debut in 2022. The first release from the new deal, Madame X—Music from the Theater Xperience (Live), hit digital stores on 8 October 2021 So, just like a prayer, Madonna came back to Warner and it felt like home.

Into the Groove-Madonna's Fifty US #1 Dance Hits

'Dance is my first love so every time one of my songs is celebrated in the clubs and recognized on the charts it feels like home,' Madonna declared in 2020 whilst celebrating her fiftieth #1 on Billboard's Dance Club Songs chart in the US with 'I Don't Search I Find'.

With fifty #1s on one chart, Madonna also extended her record with no other act getting near to matching it. The closest, incidentally, is not Elvis Presley, The Beatles, or Drake, but American country music legend George Strait (with #44 Hot Country Songs #1). 'I never take the support of my fans for granted,' Madonna said respectfully, 'and it's always like the very first time.'

1983 'Holiday'/'Lucky Star' (five weeks at No. 1)
1984 'Like a Virgin' (three)
1985 'Material Girl'
1985 'Angel'/'Into the Groove'
1987 'Open Your Heart'
1987 'Causing a Commotion'
1988 You Can Dance (LP cuts)
1989 'Like a Prayer' (two)
1989 'Express Yourself' (three)
1990 'Keep It Together'
1990 'Vogue' (two)
1991 'Justify My Love' (two)
1992 'Erotica'
1993 'Deeper and Deeper'
1993 'Fever'
1994 'Secret' (two)
1995 'Bedtime Story'
1997 'Don't Cry for Me Argentina'

1998 'Frozen' (two)
1998 'Ray of Light' (four)
1999 'Nothing Really Matters' (two)
1999 'Beautiful Stranger' (two)
2000 'American Pie'
2000 'Music' (five)
2001 'Don't Tell Me'
2001 'What It Feels Like for a Girl'
2001 'Impressive Instant' (two)
2002 'Die Another Day' (two)
2003 'American Life'
2003 'Hollywood'
2003 'Me Against the Music'—Britney Spears featuring Madonna (two)
2004 'Nothing Fails'
2004 'Love Profusion'
2005 'Hung Up' (four)
2006 'Sorry' (two)
2006 'Get Together'
2006 'Jump' (two)
2008 '4 Minutes'—Madonna featuring Justin Timberlake & Timbaland (two)
2008 'Give It 2 Me'
2009 'Celebration'
2012 'Give Me All Your Luvin''—Madonna featuring Nicki Minaj & M.I.A.
2012 'Girl Gone Wild'
2012 'Turn Up the Radio'
2015 'Living for Love'
2015 'Ghosttown'
2015 'Bitch I'm Madonna'—Madonna featuring Nicki Minaj
2019 'Medellín'—Madonna & Maluma
2019 'I Rise'
2019 'Crave'—Madonna & Swae Lee
2020 'I Don't Search I Find'

(Source: Billboard magazine)

The English Rose-
Madonna's UK Hit List

Title	Year	Peak Position
'Holiday'	1984	6
'Lucky Star'	1984	14
'Borderline'	1984	56
'Like a Virgin'	1984	3
'Material Girl'	1985	3
'Crazy for You'	1985	2
'Into the Groove'	1985	1
'Holiday' (Rerelease)	1985	2
'Angel'	1985	5
'Gambler'	1985	4
'Dress You Up'	1985	5
'Borderline' (Rerelease)	1986	2
'Live to Tell'	1986	2
'Lucky Star' (Rerelease)	1986	83
'Papa Don't Preach'	1986	1
'True Blue'	1986	1
'Open Your Heart'	1986	4
'La Isla Bonita'	1987	1
'Who's That Girl'	1987	1
'Causing A Commotion'	1987	4
'The Look of Love'	1987	9
'Like a Prayer'	1989	1
'Into the Groove/Who's That Girl' (Rerelease)	1989	99
'Express Yourself'	1989	5
'Cherish'	1989	3
'Dear Jessie'	1989	5
'Vogue'	1990	1

'Hanky Panky'	1990	2
'Justify My Love'	1990	2
'Crazy for You' (Rerelease)	1991	2
'Rescue Me'	1991	3
'Holiday' (The Holiday Collection)	1991	5
'This Used to be My Playground'	1992	3
'Erotica'	1992	6
'Deeper and Deeper'	1992	6
'Bad Girl'	1993	10
'Fever'	1993	6
'Rain'	1993	7
'I'll Remember'	1994	7
'Secret'	1994	5
'Take a Bow'	1994	16
'Bedtime Story'	1995	4
'Human Nature'	1995	8
'You'll See'	1995	5
'Oh Father'	1996	16
'One More Chance'	1996	11
'You Must Love Me'	1996	10
'Don't Cry for Me Argentina'	1996	3
'Another Suitcase in Another Hall'	1997	7
'Frozen'	1998	1
'Ray of Light'	1998	2
'Drowned World (Substitute for Love)'	1998	10
'The Power of Good-bye' (Import)	1998	91
'The Power of Good-bye/Little Star'	1998	6
'Nothing Really Matters'	1999	7
'Beautiful Stranger'	1999	2
'American Pie'	2000	1
'Music'	2000	1
'Don't Tell Me'	2000	4
'What It Feels Like for a Girl'	2001	7
'Die Another Day' (Import)	2002	93
'Die Another Day'	2002	3
'American Life' (Import)	2003	57
'American Life'	2003	2
'Hollywood'	2003	2
'Me Against the Music'	2003	2
'Love Profusion'	2003	11
'Hung Up'	2005	1
'Sorry'	2006	1

'Get Together'	2006	7
'Jump'	2006	9
'4 Minutes'	2008	1
'Give It 2 Me'	2008	7
'Miles Away'	2008	39
'Celebration'	2009	3
'Give Me All Your Luvin''	2012	37
'Masterpiece'	2012	68
'Girl Gone Wild'	2012	73
'Living for Love'	2015	26
'Medellín'	2019	87
'Levitating' (Dua Lipa)	2020	39

Source: Officialcharts.com

About the Author
Addicted

Marc Andrews is a lifelong Madonna diehard and proud of it. Born in Melbourne, Australia, he worked as a writer at 'pop Bible' Smash Hits magazine in Australia from 1988–1990, then the UK Smash Hits 'mothership' edition from 1990–1992, and as editor of the Australian edition from 1992–1995.

He is the author of two Australian Madonna fanzines—1989's Madonna: The Unofficial Story and 1993's Madonna: The Material Girlie Down Under. In 2016, he contributed three articles to Classic Pop magazine's Madonna special, which has since been translated into numerous foreign-language editions.

His music writings, interviews, and reviews have appeared in numerous magazines around the world over the last four decades and he has also had stints working for 'industry Bible' Mediaweek magazine, The Daily Mail's MailOnline, and Australian gay glossy DNA magazine, where he is currently entertainment editor.

He is also the author of three books—2010's self-published novel Revelations: 2 Weeks in Tel Aviv, 2011's Pop Life: Inside Smash Hits Australia 1984–2007 with David Nichols and Claire Isaac (Affirm Press), and 2012's We Need to Talk: My Life as a Doggone Celebrity Journalist as a Kindle exclusive for Amazon.

Now based in London, Andrews resides there with his husband, their dogs, and his beloved Madonna collection.

Bibliography
Iconic

Books

Andrews, M., Isaac, C., & Nichols, D., Pop Life: Inside Smash Hits Australia 1984–2007 (Australia: Affirm Press 2011)

Ciccone, C., & Leigh, W., Life with My Sister Madonna (USA: Simon Spotlight Entertainment 2008)

Ciccone, M., Sex (USA: Warner Books 1992)

Ciccone, M., The Girlie Show (UK: Prion Books 1994)

Cornetteau, R., Jacquemin, P., & Marck, F., Madonna Collectors: The Must-Have Volume 2/The 12″ Vinyls (France: Illogical Music 2020)

Harry, D., Face It (USA: HarperCollins 2019)

Kutner, J., & Leigh, S., 1000 UK Number One Hits (UK: Omnibus 2010)

Lagerfeld, K., Madonna Superstar (USA: W.W. Norton 1988)

McKenzie, M., Lucky Star (USA: Columbus Books 1985)

Parker, A., The Making of Evita (USA: Collins 1996)

Rettenmund, M., Encyclopedia Madonnica 20 (USA: Boy Culture 2015)

Rodgers, N., Le Freak: An Upside Down Story of Family, Disco and Destiny (USA: Hachette 2011)

Interviews

Lady Gaga, David Guetta, Cyndi Lauper, Dannii Minogue, Kylie Minogue, William Orbit, Shep Pettibone, Andrea Riseborough, Joan Rivers, Neil Tennant (Pet Shop Boys), Junior Vasquez

Magazines and Newsletters

Icon—quarterly publication of the Official Madonna Fan Club (USA: 1990–2006)

Madonna: The Material Girlie Down Under (Australia: Mason Stewart 1993)

Madonna: The Unauthorized Story (Australia: Mason Stewart 1989)

Sleeve Notes, Audio Tracks, and Documentaries

GHV2 (2001); I Am Because We Are (2008); I'm Going to Tell You a Secret (2005);
Ray of Light: Words + Music US promo CD (1998); secretprojectrevolution (2013);
Something to Remember (1995); The Immaculate Collection (1990); Truth or Dare:
In Bed with Madonna (1991); World of Madame X (2019); You Can Dance (1987).

TV, Radio, News Media, and Record Labels

American Bandstand*; Attitude magazine; Billboard magazine; CD:TV; The Chicago
Sun-Times; Classic Pop magazine; Detroit News; DJ Times magazine; DNA
magazine; E!; Electronics Magazine; Ellen; Empire magazine; Entertainment
Weekly; GQ magazine; Glamour magazine; Interview Magazine; Keyboard
Magazine; Mediaweek magazine; Mojo magazine; MTV; NME; Q magazine*;
No.1 magazine*; Rolling Stone magazine; Record Collector magazine; RuPaul's
Drag Race; Sirius Radio; Smash Hits magazine* (UK and Australia editions);
Spin magazine; Têtu magazine; The Atlantic magazine; The Face* magazine; The
Guardian; The New York Times; TIME magazine; Universal Music; US Weekly;
Vanity Fair magazine; Vibe magazine*; Vice magazine; W magazine; Warner Music.
(*denotes no longer in publication or on-air)

Websites/Podcasts

Albumism; Allaboutmadonna.com; ASCAP; Billboard.com; BPI; boyculture.com;
Discogs; drownedmadonna.com; idolator.com; imdb.com; Inside The Groove
podcast; madonna.com; Madonna on Facebook; Madonna Australia on Facebook
(strike a pose, Matt Tyler!); Madonna's Empire on Facebook; madonnarama.
com; Madonna The Supreme Real Music Diva on Facebook; madonnatribe.
com; madonnaTV; madonnaunderground.com; mad-eyes.net; MailOnline;
mixwomaneblondworld.blogspot.com; muuMuse; Officialcharts.com; peterrafelson.
com; Pitchfork; rateyourmusic.com; Rollingstone.com; Slant magazine; Smash
Hits Remembered on Facebook; Sondheim.com; todayinmadonnahistory.com;
udiscovermusic.com; Vogue.com; Wikipedia.org; YouTube; web-o-rama.net/
madonnaremixology.